MW00575168

Essentials of

PERSIAN GRAMMAR

CONCEPTS AND EXERCISES

Nazanin Mirsadeghi

Bahar Books
www.baharbooks.com

Mirsadeghi, Nazanin
Essentials of Persian Grammar: Concepts and Exercises (Farsi- English Bi-lingual Edition)/Nazanin Mirsadeghi

Editor: Molly Singleton-Coyne

This book remains the property of the publisher and copyright holder, Bahar Books, LLC.
All rights reserved under International Copyright Conventions.
No part of this book may be used, distributed or reproduced in any forms or by any means without the prior written permission of the publisher.

1st Edition: ISBN-10: 1939099315 - ISBN-13: 978-1-939099-31-0

2nd Edition:
ISBN-10: 1939099455
ISBN- 13: 978-1-939099-45-7

Copyright © 2014 by Bahar Books, LLC

Published by Bahar Books, White Plains, New York

Essentials of

PERSIAN GRAMMAR

CONCEPTS AND EXERCISES

Contents

Preface... 11

Persian Language and Script... 12

Table A: Pronouncing Persian Letters................................... 13

Table B: Names of Persian Letters.. 17

Table C: Persian Numbers.. 19

CHAPTER 1: NOUNS... 23

    Simple Nouns.. 23

    Compound Nouns.. 23

    Nouns Derived from the Present Stem of a Verb.............. 24

    Nouns Derived from the Past Stem of a Verb.................. 24

    Proper Nouns.. 25

    Common Nouns... 25

    Definite Nouns.. 26

    Indefinite Nouns.. 27

    Singular Nouns.. 29

    Plural Nouns.. 30

Chapter 1- Vocabulary... 33

Chapter 1- Test Yourself.. 36

CHAPTER 2: PRONOUNS.. 48

    Personal Pronouns... 48

        Pronouns as Subjects... 49

        Pronouns as Direct Objects..................................... 49

        Pronouns as Indirect Objects................................... 52

        Possessive Pronouns.. 54

        Common Reflexive Pronouns.................................... 58

Personal Reflexive Pronouns..................................... 58

Table 2.1: Personal Pronouns Summary..................... 60

Table 2.2: Personal Pronouns Summary..................... 61

Demonstrative Pronouns.. 62

Indefinite Pronouns.. 64

Interrogative Pronouns... 65

Chapter 2- Vocabulary.. 67

Chapter 2- Test Yourself.. 71

CHAPTER 3: ADJECTIVES... 86

Simple Adjectives... 86

Compound Adjectives.. 86

Descriptive Adjectives... 87

Adjective of Relation... 87

Adjectives Derived from the Present Stem of a Verb...... 90

Adjectives Derived from the Past Stem of a Verb.......... 91

Demonstrative Adjectives.. 92

Adjectives of Number.. 94

Adjectives of Competence.. 95

Indefinite Adjectives... 96

Comparative Forms of Adjectives.............................. 96

Superlative Forms of Adjectives................................ 97

Interrogative Adjectives.. 98

Positive & Negative Adjectives................................. 98

Chapter 3- Vocabulary.. 100

Chapter 3- Test Yourself.. 105

CHAPTER 4: ADVERBS... 119

Simple Adverbs... 119

Compound Adverbs.. 119

Adverbs of Time.. 120

Adverbs of Place.. 120

Adverbs of Quantity... 120

Adverbs of Quality... 121

Descriptive Adverbs.. 121

Adverbs of Repetition... 122

Repetitive Adverbs.. 123

Adverbs of Gradation... 123

Negative Adverbs... 123

Arabic Adverbs... 123

Chapter 4- Vocabulary.. 124

Chapter 4- Test Yourself... 128

CHAPTER 5: PREPOSITIONS... 136

Simple Prepositions.. 136

Compound Prepositions.. 137

Chapter 5- Vocabulary.. 143

Chapter 5- Test Yourself... 146

CHAPTER 6: CONJUNCTIONS.. 148

Simple Conjunctions... 148

Compound Conjunctions... 149

Chapter 6- Vocabulary.. 151

Chapter 6- Test Yourself... 154

CHAPTER 7: KASRE-YE EZĂFE... 156

Chapter 7- Vocabulary.. 160

Chapter 7- Test Yourself... 162

Chapter 8- DIRECT OBJECT INDICATOR را 165

Chapter 8- Vocabulary.. 170

Chapter 8- Test Yourself... 172

CHAPTER 9: ARABIC SIGNS.. 175

Tašdid... 175

Tanvin... 176

Hamze... 176

Chapter 9- Vocabulary.. 179

Chapter 9- Test Yourself... 182

CHAPTER 10: VERBS.. 189

    The Infinitive Form of Verbs.................................. 189

    Simple Verbs.. 190

    Compound Verbs.. 190

    Prefix Verbs... 190

    Phrasal Verbs... 190

    Verb Tenses... 191

        Simple Present.. 191

        Present Subjunctive..................................... 192

        Present Progressive..................................... 193

        Simple Past... 194

        Imperfect Indicative.................................... 194

        Present Perfect.. 195

        Past Perfect.. 195

        Past Subjunctive... 196

        Past Progressive... 196

        Simple Future.. 197

        Command... 197

    Elements of a Simple Verb.................................... 198

        Tense Prefixes... 199

        Present Stems or Past Stems......................... 199

        Personal Suffixes (Endings).......................... 200

    Regular and Irregular Verbs.................................. 202

    Stems of the Verb.. 202

        Present Stems of Regular Verbs.................... 203

        Present Stems of Irregular Verbs.................. 204

        Table 10.1: Present Stems of Irregular Verbs...... 204

        Past Stems of Regular Verbs........................ 206

        Past Stems of Irregular Verbs...................... 207

    Past Participles.. 208

    Auxiliary Verbs.. 208

Table 10.2: Conjugation of کردن **(to do) in eleven tenses....**   **210**

Transitive Verbs and Intransitive Verbs................................   **220**

Dual-mood Verbs..   **221**

Active and Passive Voices...   **221**

Negative Verbs...   **223**

Table 10.3: Tense Prefixes (Positive and Negative)..............   **226**

Chapter 10- Vocabulary...   **228**

Chapter 10- Test Yourself..   **233**

Key to the Exercises...   **256**

References...   **269**

Preface

The "Essentials of Persian Grammar" is designed to assist learners of Persian language to better understand the most important elements of Persian grammar.

This is not a text book. It is a resource to support Persian language learners and to supplement primary sources for students of Persian language.

Each chapter is dedicated to an essential element of Persian grammar providing clear explanations and multiple examples followed by applied exercises. There are more than 100 pages of exercises throughout the book, with the solution keys available at the end of the book.

All examples and exercises are accompanied by their English translations and the transliteration of the Persian words and sentences.

In order to understand the material presented in this book, you must have some basic knowledge of writing and reading in Persian; however, in the beginning of the book, a brief overview of the Persian alphabet and the pronunciation of Persian letters have been provided.

The goal of this book is to help those who are learning the Persian language methodically advance their language skills.

A special thanks to Molly Singleton-Coyne for her diligent work as the editor of this book.

Nazanin Mirsadeghi

The Persian Language and Script

The Persian language is more than twelve hundred years old and comes from the family of Indo-European languages. Indo-European languages have branched all over the globe from Europe to a vast part of Asia, the Americas and Southern portions of the African continent.

Similar to other languages, the Persian language has evolved throughout the centuries and what we know today as the modern Persian language is the latest stage of this transformation.

Persian is written on the page from right to left. Though the Persian language is unrelated to Arabic in its origin, the Arabic script is used in Persian writing. The Persian alphabet consists of 32 letters. There are no capital letters and no gender distinctions for words.

You will find a brief overview of Persian letters, their names and correct pronunciations in the following tables.

Pronouncing Persian Letters – Table A

ă like the "**a**" in arm	‌* آ– ا
b like the "**b**" in boy	ب – بـ
p like the "**p**" in play	پ – پـ
t like the "**t**" in tree	ت – تـ
s like the "**s**" in sun	ث – ثـ
j like the "**j**" in jam	ج – جـ
č like the "**ch**" in child	چ – چـ
h like the "**h**" in hotel	ح – حـ
ǩ like "**ch**" in the German word *bach*, or Hebrew word *smach*.	خ – خـ
d like the "**d**" in door	د
z like the "**z**" in zebra	ذ
r like the "**r**" in rabbit	ر
z like the "**z**" in zebra	ز
ž like the "**z**" in zwago	ژ
s like the "**s**" in sun	س – سـ

š like the **"sh"** in **sh**ell	ش - شـ
s like the **"s"** in **s**un	ص - صـ
z like the **"z"** in **z**ebra	ض- ضـ
t like the **"t"** in **t**ree	ط
z like the **"z"** in **z**ebra	ظ
' is a glottal stop, like between the syllables of "uh-oh".	ع - عـ - ـعـ - ـع
ğ like the **"r"** in French word *merci*	غ - غـ - ـغـ - ـغ
f like the **"f"** in **f**all	ف - فـ
ǧ like the **"r"** in French word *merci*	ق - قـ
k like the **"k"** in **k**ite	ک - کـ
g like the **"g"** in **g**ame	گ - گـ
l like the **"l"** in **l**ost	ل - لـ
m like the **"m"** in **m**aster	م - مـ
n like the **"n"** in **n**ight	ن - نـ
v like the **"v"** in **v**an	و
o like the **"o"** in **o**cean	و

On some occasions, it has no sound and becomes silent.	و
u like the **"u"** in sure	* او ‌- و
h like the **"h"** in hotel	هـ ‌- ‌ـهـ ‌- ‌ـه ‌- ه
e like the **"e"** in element	ـه ‌- ه
y like the **"y"** in yellow	یـ ‌- ی
i like the **"ee"** in need	* ایـ ‌- ‌یـ ‌- ‌ی‌-‌ای

      *   long vowels

a like the **"a"** in animal	ـٰ ‌- آ **
o like the **"o"** in ocean	ـُ ‌- أ **
e like the **"e"** in element	ـِ ‌- ا **

      ** short vowels

Arabic Signs

Represents doubled consonants.	ـّ
' is a glottal stop, like between the syllables of "uh-oh".	ء
an like **"an"** in the "can"	ـً

Persian Letters with the Same Pronunciation

(extracted from Table A)

t like the **"t"** in tree	ت – ﺗ
	ط
ğ like the **"r"** in French word *merci*	ق – ﻗ
	غ – ﻍ – ﻐ – ﻏ
h like the **"h"** in hotel	ح – ﺣ
	ﻫ – ﻬ – ﻪ – ه
s like the **"s"** in sun	ث – ﺛ
	س – ﺳ
	ص – ﺻ
z like the **"z"** in zebra	ذ
	ز
	ض – ﺿ
	ظ

Names of Persian Letters– Table B

alef	آ– ا
be	ب – بـ
pe	پ – پـ
te	ت – تـ
se	ث – ثـ
jim	ج – جـ
če	چ – چـ
he	ح – حـ
ǩe	خ – خـ
dǎl	د
zǎl	ذ
re	ر
ze	ز
že	ژ
sin	س – سـ
šin	ش – شـ

săd	صـ – ص
zăd	ضـ – ض
tă	ط
ză	ظ
eyn	عـ – ـعـ – ـع – ع
ğeyn	غـ – ـغـ – ـغ – غ
fe	فـ – ف
ğăf	قـ – ق
kăf	كـ – ك
găf	گـ – گ
lăm	لـ – ل
mim	مـ – م
noon	نـ – ن
văv	و
he	هـ – ـهـ – ـه – ه
ye	یـ – ی

Persian Numbers– Table C

one	1	۱	یک
two	2	۲	دو
three	3	۳	سه
four	4	۴	چهار
five	5	۵	پنج
six	6	۶	شش
seven	7	۷	هفت
eight	8	۸	هشت
nine	9	۹	نه
ten	10	۱۰	ده
eleven	11	۱۱	یازده
twelve	12	۱۲	دوازده
thirteen	13	۱۳	سیزده
fourteen	14	۱۴	چهارده
fifteen	15	۱۵	پانزده

sixteen	16	۱۶	شانزده
seventeen	17	۱۷	هفده
eighteen	18	۱۸	هیجده
nineteen	19	۱۹	نوزده
twenty	20	۲۰	بیست
thirty	30	۳۰	سی
forty	40	۴۰	چهل
fifty	50	۵۰	پنجاه
sixty	60	۶۰	شصت
seventy	70	۷۰	هفتاد
eighty	80	۸۰	هشتاد
ninety	90	۹۰	نود
(one)hundred	100	۱۰۰	صد
two hundred	200	۲۰۰	دویست
three hundred	300	۳۰۰	سیصد
four hundred	400	۴۰۰	چهارصد
five hundred	500	۵۰۰	پانصد

six hundred	600	۶۰۰	ششصد
seven hundred	700	۷۰۰	هفتصد
eight hundred	800	۸۰۰	هشتصد
nine hundred	900	۹۰۰	نهصد
(one)thousand	1000	۱۰۰۰	هزار

CHAPTER 1

NOUNS

اسم ها
‍/esm.hă/

A noun is a person, a place, a thing, or an idea. Nouns may be categorized in different ways. They may generally be classified as either *"simple nouns"* or *"compound nouns"*.

- Simple Nouns:
These nouns take the form of one word.

EXAMPLES:

sea   /dar.yă/   دریا

book   /ke.tăb/   کتاب

table/desk   /miz/   میز

- Compound Nouns:
These nouns take the form of more than one word.

EXAMPLES:

flowerpot /gol.dăn/ گُلدان (گُل + دان)

library /ke.tăb.ḱă.ne/ کتابخانه (کتاب + خانه)

fight /za.do.ḱord/ زد و خورد (زد + و + خورد)

psychology /ra.văn.še.nă.si/ روانشناسی (روان + شناس + ی)

Nouns may also be divided into the following two groups:

1) Nouns derived from the present stem of a verb:
These nouns are usually made by adding one of the following suffixes to the end of the present stem.

❖ ش ِ :
/eš/

EXAMPLES:

request /ḱă.heš/ خواهِش (خواه + ِ ش)

reduction /kă.heš/ کاهِش (کاه + ِ ش)

teaching /ă.mu.zeš/ آموزِش (آموز + ِ ش)

❖ ه — ۀ :
/e/

EXAMPLES:

laugh /ḱan.de/ خنده (خند + ه)

cry /ger.ye/ گریه (گری + ۀ)

kiss /bu.se/ بوسه (بوس + ۀ)

2) Nouns derived from the past stem of a verb:

24

These nouns are usually made by adding the suffix: ار /ăr/ to the end of the past stem.

∻ ار :

/ăr/

EXAMPLES:

speech /gof.tăr/ گفتار (گفت + ار)

killing /koš.tăr/ کُشتار (کُشت + ار)

writing /ne.veš.tăr/ نوشتار (نوشت + ار)

Nouns may also be classified as either *proper nouns* or *common nouns* based on their function and meaning in the sentence:

1) Proper Nouns:
These nouns identify a specific person, place or thing.

EXAMPLES:

Iran /i.răn/ ایران

Himalaya /hi.mă.li.yă/ هیمالیا

Shakespeare /šeks.pir/ شکسپیر

2) Common Nouns:
These nouns identify people, places and things in general.

EXAMPLES:

ocean /o.ği.yă.nus/ اُقیانوس

police/policeman /po.lis/ پُلیس

street /ăi.yă.băn/ خیابان

Nouns may also be classifies as either *definite nouns* or *indefinite nouns* based on their function and meaning in the sentence:

1) Definite Nouns:

If the noun is known to the *persons or things speaking* or to the *persons or things spoken to*, it is called a *definite noun*. There is no article for *definite nouns* in the Persian language.

EXAMPLES:

سارا کتاب را به من داد.

/să.ră- ke.tăb- ră- be- man- dăd/

Sara gave me the book.

آنها خیابان را به من نشان دادند.

/ăn.hă- ǩi.yă.băn- ră- be- man-ne.šăn- dă.dand/

They showed me the street.

Note:

All proper nouns are definite nouns:

EXAMPLE:

شوهرم مریم را می شناسد.

/šo.ha.ram- mar.yam- ră- mi.še.nă.sad/

My husband knows Maryam.

Note:

The subjects of all demonstrative adjectives are definite nouns:

EXAMPLE:

آن گلدان را به من بده !

/ăn- gol.dăn- ră- be- man- be.de/

Give me that flowerpot!

Note:

All concrete, abstract and material nouns are definite nouns:

EXAMPLES:

من باران را دوست دارم !

/man- bă.răn- ră- dust- dă.ram/

I like the rain!

حقیقت اهمّیت دارد !

/ha.ği.ğat- a.ham.mi.yat- dă.rad/
Truth matters!

فولاد از آهن محکم تر است.

/fu.lăd- az- ă.han- moh.kam.tar- ast/
Steel is stronger than iron.

2) Indefinite Nouns:

If the noun is unknown to the *persons or things speaking* or to the *persons or things spoken to*, it is called an *indefinite noun*. The indefinite articles in the Persian language are:

- the suffix ی /i/ which is added to the end of nouns in either singular or plural form.

- the word یک /yek/, which comes only before a singular noun.

- the suffix ی /i/ and the word یک /yek/ which are used after and before a noun in the case of singular nouns only. This form is usually used in conversations as opposed to writing.

EXAMPLES:

- with the suffix ی /i/:

آنها خیابانی را به من نشان دادند.

/ăn.hă- ǩi.yă.bă.ni- ră- be- man- ne.šăn- dă.dand/
They showed me a street.

دخترانی را دیدم که گُل می فروختند.

/doǩ.ta.ră-ni- ră- di.dam- ke- gol- mi.fo.ruǩ.tand/
I saw some girls who were selling flowers.

- with the word یک /yek/ (coming before the noun):

27

یک نفر را دیدم که در خیابان راه می رفت.

/yek- na.far- ră- di.dam- ke- dar- ǐi.yă.băn- răh- mi.raft/

I saw <u>a person</u> walking in the street.

یک گربه کنارِ پنجره خوابیده بود.

/yek- gor.be- ke.nă.re- pan.je.re- ǩă.bi.de- bud/

<u>A cat</u> was sleeping next to the window.

- with both the suffix ی /i/ and the word یک /yek/:

یک پلیسی را دیدم که تو را می شناخت.

/yek- po.li.si- ră- di.dam- ke- to- ră- mi.še.năǩt/

I saw <u>a policeman</u> who knew you.

یک دختری پُستخانه را به من نشان داد.

/yek- doǩ.ta.ri- post.ǩă.ne- ră- be- man- ne.šăn- dăd/

<u>A girl</u> showed me the post office.

Note:

If the noun ends in ه — ه with the /e/ sound, the suffix ی /i/ changes

into ای /i/.

EXAMPLES:

شوهرم برایِ ما ترانه ای خواند.

/šo.ha.ram- ba.ră.ye- mă- ta.ră.ne.i- ǩănd/

My husband sang <u>a song</u> for us.

سارا به من هدیه ای داد.

/să.ră- be- man- had.ye.i- dăd/

Sara gave me <u>a gift</u>.

Keep in Mind: The above rule only applies to words ending in ه — ـه with the /e/ sound, not to words ending in the letter ه — ـه with the /h/ sound.

EXAMPLES:

an excuse   /ba.hǎ.ne.i/   بهانه ای (بهانه + ای)

a seed   /dǎ.ne.i/   دانه ای (دانه + ای)

a hill   /tap.pe.i/   تپّه ای (تپّه + ای)

vs.

a way   /rǎ.hi/   راهی (راه + ی)

a mountain   /ku.hi/   کوهی (کوه + ی)

a month/a moon   /mǎ.hi/   ماهی (ماه + ی)

Note:

If the noun ends in the letter ا /ǎ/ or in the letter و /u/, the suffix ی /i/ changes into یی /yi/.

EXAMPLES:

من صدایی می شنوم.

/man- se.dǎ.yi- mi.še.na.vam/
I hear a sound.

آنها آهویی دیدند.

/ǎn.hǎ- ǎ.hu.yi- di.dand/
They saw a deer.

Nouns may also be classified as either *singular nouns* or *plural nouns*:

1) Singular Nouns:
These nouns refer to one person, place, or thing.

EXAMPLES:

tree   /de.rak̆t/   درخت

house   /k̆ă.ne/   خانه

2) Plural Nouns:
These nouns refer to more than one person, place or thing.
The plural is formed by one of the following:

a) The suffix   ها   /hă/   may be added to the end of all singular nouns to form plural.

EXAMPLES:

trees   /de.rak̆t.hă/   درخت ها (درخت + ها)

houses/homes   /k̆ă.ne.hă/   خانه ها (خانه + ها)

b) For some nouns the plural can also be formed by adding the suffix   ان   /ăn/   to the end of the singular noun.

EXAMPLES:

trees   /de.rak̆.tăn/   درختان (درخت + ان)

girls/daughters   /dok̆.ta.răn/   دختران (دختر + ان)

   Note:

   If the singular noun ends in the letter   ا   /ă/ , the plural suffix   ان   /ăn/ changes into

   یان   /yăn/.

   EXAMPLE:

   gentlemen   /ă.ğă.yăn/   آقایان ⟵ (یان) ان + آقا

   Note:

   If the singular noun ends in the letter   و   /u/ , the plural suffix   ان   /ăn/ may change to

   یان   /yăn/.

30

EXAMPLE:

students /dă.neš.ju.yǎn/ دانشجویان ← (یان) ان + دانشجو

> **Keep in Mind:** Some singular nouns ending in the letter و /u/ follow the general rule when it comes to adding the suffix ان /ǎn/, but the pronunciation of the letter و changes from /u/ into /ov/.

EXAMPLES:

ladies /bǎ.no.vǎn/ بانوان (ان + بانو)

deer /ǎ.ho.vǎn/ آهوان (ان + آهو)

> **Note:**

If the singular noun ends in ه — ـه with the /e/ sound, the ه — ـه changes into گ /g/ and joins the plural suffix ان /ǎn/.

EXAMPLES:

writers /ne.vi.san.de.ğǎn/ نویسندگان ← (گان) ان + نویسنده

singers /ǩǎ.nan.de.ğǎn/ خوانندگان ← (گان) ان + خواننده

c) The suffix جات /jǎt/ may be added to the end of certain nouns to form plural.

EXAMPLES:

vegetables/herbs /sab.zi.jǎt/ سبزیجات (سبزی + جات)

fruits /mi.ve.jǎt/ میوه جات (میوه + جات)

pastries /ši.ri.ni.jǎt/ شیرینی جات (شیرینی + جات)

d) Some Arabic plurals are formed by adding the suffix ات /ǎt/ to the end of certain nouns.

Examples:

animals /hey.vă.năt/ حيوانات (حيوان + ات)

repairs /taʻ.mi.răt/ تعميرات (تعمير + ات)

e) Most Arabic nouns have irregular plural forms.

Examples:

numbers /aʻ.dăd/ أَعداد ← عدد

waves /am.văj/ أَمواج ← موج

types /an.văʻ/ أَنواع ← نوع

Chapter 1- Vocabulary

آ

sky	آسمان
gentleman/Mr.	آقا
teaching	آموزش
they/them	آنها
iron	آهن
deer	آهو

ا

name/noun	اسم
ocean	اقیانوس
to matter	اهمّیت داشتن
Iran	ایران

ب

rain	باران
lady	بانو
kiss	بوسه
to	به
excuse	بهانه

پ

post office	پستخانه
police/policeman	پلیس
window	پنجره

ت

hill	تپّه
song	ترانه
repair	تعمیر
you	تو

ح

truth	حقیقت
animal	حیوان

خ

house/home	خانه
laugh	خنده
to sleep	خوابیدن
to read	خواندن
singer/reader	خواننده
request	خواهش
street	خیابان

د

to give	دادن
student	دانشجو
seed	دانه
girl/daughter	دختر
in	در
about	درباره ی
tree	درخت
to shine	درخشیدن
sea	دریا

NOUNS

to like/ to love	دوست داشتن
to see	دیدن

ر

way	راه
to walk	راه رفتن
psychology	روانشناسی
on/ over	رویِ

ز

fight	زد و خورد

س

vegetable/herb	سبزی

ش

Shakespeare	شکسپیر
to break	شکستن
to know	شناختن
to hear	شنیدن
husband	شوهر
pastry	شیرینی

ص

sound	صدا

ع

number	عدد

ف

to sell	فروختن
steel	فولاد

ک

reduction	کاهش
book	کتاب
library	کتابخانه
killing	کشتار
next to	کنارِ
mountain	کوه

گ

cat	گربه
cry	گریه
speech	گفتار
flower	گُل
flowerpot	گُلدان

م

we/us	ما
month/ moon	ماه
stronger	محکم تر
I/me	من
wave	موج
table/desk	میز
fruit	میوه

34

ن

to show	نشان دادن
person	نفر
writing	نوشتار
type	نوع
writer	نویسنده

ه

gift	هدیه
Himalaya	هیمالیا

Test Yourself:

1.1 Look at the words below. Find the **compound nouns** in the list and write each of their elements in the spaces provided. There are 5 **compound nouns** in this exercise.

month/moon   /măh/ **ماه**

flowerpot   /gol.dăn/ **گلدان**

psychology   /ra.văn.še.nă.si/ **روانشناسی**

cat   /gor.be/ **گربه**

Sara   /să.ră/ **سارا**

mountain   /kuh/ **کوه**

gift   /had.ye/ **هدیه**

I/me   /man/ **من**

sea   /dar.yă/ **دریا**

library   /ke.tăb.kă.ne/ **کتابخانه**

America   /ăm.ri.kă/ **آمریکا**

sound   /se.dă/ **صدا**

شوهر /šo.har/ husband

کتاب /ke.tăb/ book

تهران /teh.răn/ Tehran

میز /miz/ table/desk

پلیس /po.lis/ police/policeman

زد و خورد /za.do.ǩord/ fight

پنجره /pan.je.re/ window

راه /răh/ way

درخت /de.raǩt/ tree

پستخانه /post.ǩă.ne/ post office

Example: ۱– گُل + دان

۲– _____ + _____ + _____

۳– _____ + _____

۴– _____ + _____ + _____

NOUNS

─── + ─── ۵–

1.2 Find the **nouns** in the sentences below and write them on the lines. The number of **nouns** in each sentence is indicated in parentheses.

Example:

۱– سارا میوه دوست دارد. (۲)

/să.ră- mi.ve- dust- dă.rad/
Sara likes fruit.

میوه ـــــــ سارا ـــــــ

۲– کتاب ها روی میز هستند. (۲)

/ke.tăb.hă- ru.ye- miz- has.tand/
The books are on the table.

ـــــــ ـ ـــــــ

۳– خانه ی سینا در تهران نیست. (۳)

/kă.ne.ye- si.nă- dar- teh.răn- nist/
Sina's house is not in Tehran.

ـــــ ـ ـــــ ـ ـــــ

۴– خنده ی سارا را دوست دارم. (۲)

/kan.de.ye- să.ră- ră- dust- dă.ram/
[I] like Sara's laugh.

ـــــ ـ ـــــ

38

۵– روی میز سارا، کتابی درباره ی هیمالیا دیدم. (۴)

/ru.ye- mi.ze- să.ră- ke.tă.bi- dar.bă.re.ye- hi.mă.li.yă- di.dam/

[I] found a book about Himalaya on Sara's desk.

_____   _____   _____   _____

۶– گلدان دخترم شکست. (۲)

/gol.dă.ne- dok̆.ta.ram- še.kast/

My daughter's flowerpot broke.

_____   _____

۷– ماه در آسمان تهران می درخشد. (۳)

/măh- dar- ă.se.mă.ne- teh.răn- mi.de.rak̆.šad/

The moon is shining in Tehran's sky.

_____   _____   _____

۸– خیابان ما درخت ندارد. (۲)

/k̆i.yă.bă.ne- mă- de.rak̆t- na.dă.rad/

There are no trees in our street.

_____   _____

NOUNS

1.3 Each of these nouns has at least one **plural form**. Write the appropriate **plural forms** for each noun in the spaces provided.

Example: girl/daughter /doǩ.tar/ **دختر** – ۱

دختران ، دخترها

animal /jǎ.ne.var/ **جانور** – ۲

_____ ، _____

vegetable/herb /sab.zi/ **سبزی** – ۳

_____ ، _____

tree /de.raǩt/ **درخت** – ۴

_____ ، _____

number /ʻa.dad/ **عدد** – ۵

_____ ، _____

singer/reader /kǎ.nan.de/ خواننده ‎-۶

‗‗‗‗‗‗‗‗‗‗ ‚ ‗‗‗‗‗‗‗‗‗‗

wave /moj/ موج ‎-۷

‗‗‗‗‗‗‗‗‗‗ ‚ ‗‗‗‗‗‗‗‗‗‗

writer /ne.vi.san.de/ نویسنده ‎-۸

‗‗‗‗‗‗‗‗‗‗ ‚ ‗‗‗‗‗‗‗‗‗‗

month/moon /mǎh/ ماه ‎-۹

‗‗‗‗‗‗‗‗‗‗

song /ta.rǎ.ne/ ترانه ‎-۱۰

‗‗‗‗‗‗‗‗‗‗

1.4 On the lines next to the following words, indicate whether it is a **common noun** by writing *"cn"* or a **proper noun** by writing *"pn"*. There are 9 **proper nouns** and 12 **common nouns** in this exercise.

Example: *cn*   student /dǎ.neš.ju/ دانشجو

NOUNS

_____ house/home /ǩă.ne/ **خانه**

_____ Elizabeth /e.li.ză.bet/ **الیزابت**

_____ France /fa.răn.se/ **فرانسه**

_____ flower /gol/ **گُل**

_____ animal /hey.văn/ **حیوان**

_____ Sara /să.ră/ **سارا**

_____ Mexico /mek.zik/ **مکزیک**

_____ April /far.var.din/ **فروردین**

_____ husband /šo.har/ **شوهر**

_____ table/desk /miz/ **میز**

_____ month/moon /măh/ **ماه**

_____ Paris /pă.ris/ **پاریس**

_____ girl/daughter /doǩ.tar/ **دختر**

_____ lady /bă.nu/ **بانو**

42

_____ Christmas /ke.ris.mas/ کریسمس

_____ window /pan.je.re/ پنجره

_____ street /ǩi.yǎ.bǎn/ خیابان

_____ New York /ni.yu.york/ نیویورک

_____ song /ta.rǎ.ne/ ترانه

_____ Norouz/Norooz /no.ruz/ نوروز

1.5 Look at the list of nouns below. Indicate the 7 nouns that are derived from the **present or past stem of a verb** by placing a check mark on the lines that precede them.

_____ cat /gor.be/ گربه

_____ seed /dǎ.ne/ دانه

Example: ____✓____ speech /gof.tǎr/ گفتار

_____ laugh /ǩan.de/ خنده

_____ table/desk /miz/ میز

NOUNS

_____ singer/reader /k̆ǎ.nan.de/ **خواننده**

_____ song /ta.rǎ.ne/ **ترانه**

_____ sound /se.dǎ/ **صدا**

_____ request /k̆ǎ.heš/ **خواهِش**

_____ sea /dar.yǎ/ **دریا**

_____ reduction /kǎ.heš/ **کاهِش**

_____ cry /ger.ye/ **گریه**

_____ tree /de.rak̆t/ **درخت**

_____ mountain /kuh/ **کوه**

_____ writing /ne.veš.tǎr/ **نوشتار**

_____ ocean /o.ği.yǎ.nus/ **اقیانوس**

_____ Shakespeare /šeks.pir/ **شکسپیر**

_____ iron /ǎ.han/ **آهن**

1.6 Change the **definite nouns** below into **indefinite nouns** and rewrite them in the spaces provided. Some words may be written in multiple ways.

Example: cat /gor.be/ گربه –۱

گربه ای   یک گربه   یک گربه ای

house/home /kǎ.ne/ خانه –۲

_____   _____   _____

tree /de.rakt/ درخت –۳

_____   _____   _____

table/desk /miz/ میز –۴

_____   _____   _____

sea /dar.yǎ/ دریا –۵

_____   _____   _____

۶- دختران /dok̆.ta.răn/ girls/daughters

_____

۷- نویسندگان /ne.vi.san.de.găn/ writers

_____

۸- کوه /kuh/ mountain

_____ _____ _____

۹- بوسه /bu.se/ kiss

_____ _____ _____

۱۰- کتاب ها /ke.tăb.hă/ books

_____

۱۱- گریه /ger.ye/ cry

_____ _____ _____

١٢ – تپّه‏ /tap.pe/ hill

_____ _____ _____

١٣ – پنجره ها‏ /pan.je.re.hă/ windows

_____

١۴ – اسم ها‏ /esm.hă/ names/nouns

_____

١۵ – سبزیجات‏ /sab.zi.jăt/ vegetables/herbs

_____

١۶ – خنده‏ /ǩan.de/ laugh

_____ _____ _____

CHAPTER 2

PRONOUNS

ضَميرها

/za.mir.hă/

Pronouns are words used in place of a noun. There are four groups of pronouns:

1) *personal pronouns*   2) *demonstrative pronouns*
3) *indefinite pronouns*   4) *interrogative pronouns*

1) Personal Pronouns:

This type of pronoun indicates which one of these three groups is being referred to: the "persons or things speaking", the "persons or things spoken to" or the "persons or things spoken of".

Personal pronouns have two forms: *detached* and *attached*.

- *Detached personal pronouns* are pronouns that can be used without other words.

- *Attached personal pronouns* are pronouns that can not be used without a noun or a verb. They are attached to the end of a noun, or a verb in a sentence.

Personal pronouns may be divided into six groups based on their function in the sentence:

a) *pronouns as subjects*   b) *pronouns as direct objects*
c) *pronouns as indirect objects*   d) *possessive pronouns*
e) *common reflexive pronouns* f) *personal reflexive pronouns*

a) Pronouns as Subjects:

These pronouns can act as the *subject* of a sentence and they are always *detached*.

– There are six *"pronouns as subjects"*:

(I) /man/   مَن

(You *sing.*) /to/ تو

(He/She) /u/ او

(We) /mǎ/ ما

(You *pl.*) /šo.mǎ/ شُما

(They) /i.šǎn/ - /ǎn.hǎ/ ایشان (آنها)

EXAMPLES:

او آمد.

/u- ǎ.mad/
He/She came.

ما در نیویورک زندگی می کنیم.

/mǎ- dar- ni.yu.york- zen.de.gi- mi.ko.nim/
We live in New York.

آنها خوابیده اند.

/ǎn.hǎ- kǎ.bi.de.and/
They are sleeping.

b) Pronouns as Direct Objects:

These pronouns can act as a *direct object* in the sentence. They could be *attached* or *detached*.

49

– There are six *"detached pronouns as direct objects"*:

(me) /man/ مَن

(you *sing.*) /to/ تو

(him/her) /u/ او

(us) /mǎ/ ما

(you *pl.*) /šo.mǎ/ شُما

(them) /i.šǎn/ - /ǎn.hǎ/ ایشان (آنها)

Note:

The *"direct object indicator"* را /rǎ/ comes after all *detached pronoun as direct objects*, to indicate the objective role of these pronouns in the sentence.

EXAMPLES:

من او را بوسیدم.

/man- u- rǎ- bu.si.dam/
I kissed <u>him/her</u>.

سارا آنها را شناخت.

/sǎ.rǎ- ǎn.hǎ- rǎ- še.nǎ̆kt/
Sara recognized <u>them</u>.

ما تو را در پارک ندیدیم.

/mǎ- to- rǎ- dar- pǎrk- na.di.dim/
We didn't see <u>you</u> in the park.

– There are six *"attached pronouns as direct objects"*, which are attached to the end of a simple verb:

50

(me) /am/ مَ

(you *sing.*) /at/ تَ

(him/her) /aš/ شَ

(us) /e.măn/ مان

(you *pl.*) /e.tăn/ تان

(them) /e.šăn/ شان

EXAMPLES:

من بوسیدمَش.

/man- bu.si.da.maš/

I kissed <u>him/her</u>.

سارا شناختشان.

/să.ră- še.năk̆.te.šăn/

Sara recognized <u>them</u>.

ما در پارک ندیدیمَت.

/mă- dar- părk- na.di.di.mat/

We didn't see <u>you</u> in the park.

Note:

In the case of *compound verbs*, *prefix verbs* and *phrasal verbs*, the *"attached pronouns as direct objects"* may be connected to the main verb or, alternatively, to the *prefixes*, *prepositions*, *nouns* and other elements of these types of verbs.

EXAMPLES:

- for *"compound verbs"*:

مویم خیس بود، خشک کردمَش.

/mu.yam- k̆is- bud- k̆ošk- kar.da.maš/

My hair was wet; [I] dried <u>it</u>.

مویم خیس بود، خشگَش کردم.

/mu.yam- k̆is- bud- k̆oš.kaš- kar.dam/

My hair was wet; [I] dried <u>it</u>.

- for *"prefix verbs"*:

کتاب هایم روی میز هستند، بردارِشان!

/ke.tăb.hă.yam- ru.ye- miz- has.tand- bar.dă.re.šăn/

My books are on the table; pick <u>them</u> up!

کتاب هایم روی میز هستند، برِشان دار!

/ke.tăb.hă.yam- ru.ye- miz- has.tand- ba.re.šăn- dăr/

My books are on the table; pick <u>them</u> up!

- for *"phrasal verbs"*:

مدیر خوبی داشتیم، امّا از دست دادیمَش.

/mo.di.re- ǩu.bi- dăš.tim- am.mă- az- dast- dă.di.maš/

We had a good manager, but we lost <u>him/her</u>.

مدیر خوبی داشتیم، امّا از دستَش دادیم.

/mo.di.re- ǩu.bi- dăš.tim- am.mă- az- das.taš- dă.dim/

We had a good manager, but we lost <u>him/her</u>.

c) Pronouns as Indirect Objects:

These pronouns can act as an *indirect object* in the sentence. They may be *attached* or *detached*. The attached forms are often seen only in poetry and classical literature. The detached forms are used in the modern literature, writing and every day conversations.

– There are six *Detached Pronouns as Indirect Objects*:

(me) /man/ مَن

(you *sing.*) /to/ تو

(him/her) /u/ او

(us) /mă/ ما

(you *pl.*) /šo.mă/ شُما

(them) /i.šăn/ - /ăn.hă/ (آنها) ایشان

Note:

Detached pronouns as indirect objects always follow one of the following prepositions:

(to)	/be/	به
(for)	/ba.ră.ye/	برایِ
(from)	/az/	از

EXAMPLES:

من به او گفتم.

/man- be- u- gof.tam/
I told <u>him/her</u>.

مادرم برایِ تو نامه نوشت.

/mă.da.ram- ba.ră.ye- to- nă.me- ne.vešt/
My mother wrote <u>you</u> a letter.

من از آنها چندین بار پرسیدم.

/man- az- ăn.hă- čan.din- băr- por.si.dam/
I asked <u>them</u> several times.

– There are six *attached pronouns as indirect objects*. They are usually used in poetry and classical literature and are attached to the end of the simple verb in a sentence:

(me)	/am/	مَ
(you *sing.*)	/at/	تَ
(him/her)	/aš/	شَ
(us)	/e.măn/	مان
(you *pl.*)	/e.tăn/	تان
(them)	/e.šăn/	شان

EXAMPLE:

در میانِ اشک ها پرسیدمَش: خوش ترین لبخند چیست؟   (هوشنگ ابتهاج)

/dar-mi.yă.ne- ašk.hă- por.si.da.maš- ǩoš.ta.rin- lab.ǩand- čist/

In the midst of tears, I asked <u>her</u>: *What's the sweetest of all smiles?*

(extracted from a poem by: Houshang Ebtehaj)

Note:

In the case of *compound verbs* the *"attached pronouns as indirect objects"* may be connected to the main verb or, alternatively, to the *nouns* or other elements related to this type of verb.

EXAMPLES:

من یاد دادمَت.

/man- yăd- dă.da.mat/

I taught <u>you</u>.

من یادَت دادم.

/man- yă.dat- dă.dam/

I taught <u>you</u>.

d) Possessive Pronouns:

Possessive pronouns indicate relationship of ownership between a pronoun and a noun. They could be detached or attached. There are six *detached* and six *attached possessive pronouns* :

– The six *"detached possessive pronouns"* come after the noun in a sentence.

(my) /man/ مَن

(your *sing.*) /to/ تو

(his/her) /u/ او

(our) /mă/ ما

(your *pl.*) /šo.mă/ شُما

(their) /i.šăn/ - /ăn.hă/ ایشان (آنها)

EXAMPLES:

دخترِ من زیباست.

/doǩ.ta.re- man- zi.bǎst/
<u>My</u> daughter is beautiful.

مادرِ ما دارد می رقصد.

/mǎ.da.re- mǎ- dǎ.rad- mi.raǧ.sad/
<u>Our</u> mother is dancing.

Note:

Detached possessive pronouns are connected to a noun by the vowel ___ /e/ *(kasre-*

ye ezǎfe). If the noun ends in the letter ا /ǎ/ , the letter و /u/ or the letter

ه — ـه /e/ , the vowel ___ changes into ی /ye/.

EXAMPLES:

کتاب های تو سنگین هستند.

/ke.tǎb.hǎ.ye- to- san.gin- has.tand/
<u>Your</u> books are heavy.

آرزوی من برآورده شد.

/ǎ.re.zu.ye- man- bar.ǎ.var.de- šod/
<u>My</u> wish came true.

خانه ی ما در این جادّه است.

/ǩǎ.ne.ye- mǎ- dar- in- jǎd.de- ast/
<u>Our</u> house is on this road.

– The six *"attached possessive pronouns"* get attached to the end of the noun:

     (my)   /am/   مَ

     (your *sing.*) /at/   تَ

(his/her) /aš/ شَ

(our) /e.măn/ مان

(your *pl.*) /e.tăn/ تان

(their) /e.šăn/ شان

EXAMPLES:

دخترَم زیباست.

/doǩ.ta.ram- zi.băst/
<u>My</u> daughter is beautiful.

کتاب هایَت سنگین هستند.

/ke.tăb.hă.yat- san.gin- has.tand/
<u>Your</u> books are heavy.

مادرمان دارد می رقصد.

/mă.da.re.măn- dă.rad- mi.raǧ.sad/
<u>Our</u> mother is dancing.

Note:

In Persian language we may use different forms of pronouns based on familiarity or formality. When talking or referring to a singular person, we may use the plural form of pronouns instead of the singular form to show respect:

❖ (شما – تان) (/e.tăn/ - /šo.mă/) instead of (تو – تَ) (/at/ - /to/)

❖ (ایشان – شان) (/e.šăn/ - /i.šăn/) instead of (او – شَ) (/aš/-/u/)

EXAMPLES:

به مادرم گفتم:"ایده ی شما بهتر است!"

/be- mă.da.ram- gof.tam- i.de.ye- šo.mă- beh.tar- ast/
[I] told my mother: "<u>Your</u> idea is better!"

به سارا گفتم: "دخترتان خیلی زیباست!"

/be- să.ră- gof.tam- dok̆.ta.re.tăn- k̆ey.li- zi.băst/

[I] told Sara: "<u>Your</u> daughter is very beautiful!"

رئیسم را دیدم و در را برای ایشان باز کردم.

/ra.ʾi.sam- ră- di.dam- va- dar- ră- ba.ră.ye- i.šăn- băz- kar.dam/

[I] saw my boss and [I] opened the door for <u>him/her</u>.

پدرم کارشان را دوست داشتند.

/pe.da.ram- kă.re.šăn- ră- dust- dăš.tand/

My father loved <u>his</u> job.

Note:

In Persian language, the *"pronominal form* of *possessive pronouns"* is shown by using the word: مال /mă.le/ which means "belong(s) to" and, it comes before *detached possessive pronouns.*

- There are six *"possessive pronouns (pronominal form)*:

    (mine) /mă.le- man/   مال من

    (yours *sing.*) /mă.le- to/   مال تو

    (his/hers) /mă.le- u/   مال او

    (ours) /mă.le- mă/   مال ما

    (yours *pl.*) /mă.le- šo.mă/   مال شما

    (theirs) /mă.le- i.šăn/- /mă.le- ăn.hă/   (مال آنها) مال ایشان

EXAMPLES:

این سیب مال من است.

/in- sib- mă.le- man- ast/

This apple is <u>mine</u>.

آن خانه مال ما بود.

/ăn- k̆ă.ne- mă.le- mă- bud/

That house was <u>ours</u>.

57

این کفش ها مال آنهاست.

/in- kafš.hǎ- mǎ.le- ǎn.hǎst/

These shoes are <u>theirs</u>.

e) Common Reflexive Pronouns:

The *common reflexive pronoun* خود /ǩod/ is used when the *subjective pronoun* and the *objective pronoun* (direct or indirect) refer to the same person.

EXAMPLE:
- for *pronoun as direct object*:

من خود را می شناسم.

/man- ǩod- rǎ- mi.še.nǎ.sam/

I know <u>myself</u>.

EXAMPLE:
- for *pronoun as indirect object*:

آنها به خود جایزه دادند.

/ǎn.hǎ- be- ǩod- jǎ.ye.ze- dǎ.dand/

They gave <u>themselves</u> presents.

Note:

The *common reflexive pronoun* خود /ǩod/ could also replace any *possessive pronoun* if the *possessive pronoun* is related to the subject of the sentence.

EXAMPLES:

سارا دخترَش را دوست دارد.

/sǎ.rǎ- doǩ.ta.raš- rǎ- dust- dǎ.rad/

Sara loves <u>her</u> daughter.

سارا دختر خود را دوست دارد.

/sǎ.rǎ- doǩ.ta.re- ǩod- rǎ- dust- dǎ.rad/

Sara loves <u>her</u> daughter.

f) Personal Reflexive Pronouns:

The *common reflexive pronoun* خود /ǩod/ could join any of the *attached objective pronouns* (direct or indirect) to form these six *personal reflexive pronouns*:

(myself) /ǩo.dam/ خودَم

(yourself *sing.*) /ǩo.dat/ خودَت

(himself/herself) /ǩo.daš/ خودَش

(ourselves) /ǩo.de.mǎn/ خودمان

(yourselves *pl.*) /ǩo.de.tǎn/ خودتان

(themselves) /ǩo.de.šǎn/ خودشان

EXAMPLE:

- for *pronouns as direct object*:

من خودم را می شناسم.

/man- ǩo.dam- rǎ- mi.še.nǎ.sam/
I know <u>myself</u>.

EXAMPLE:

- for *pronouns as indirect object*:

آنها به خودشان جایزه دادند.

/ǎn.hǎ- be- ǩo.de.šǎn- jǎ.ye.ze- dǎ.dand/
They gave <u>themselves</u> presents.

Note:
Personal reflexive pronouns may be used to emphasize "right after" or "instead of" the subject in a sentence.

EXAMPLE:

- for "right after" the subject:

سارا خودش کتاب را به من داد.

/sǎ.rǎ- ǩo.daš- ke.tǎb- rǎ- be- man- dǎd/
Sara gave me the book <u>herself</u>.

EXAMPLE:

- for "instead of" the subject:

خودم به او گفتم.

/ǩo.dam- be- u- gof.tam/
[I] told him <u>myself</u>.

Personal Pronouns (Summary)
(Table 2.1)

Pronouns as Indirect Objects	Pronouns as Direct Object		Pronouns as Subject
	Attached	Detached	
me = من	me = مَ	me = من	I = من
you *sing.* = تو	you *sing.* = تَ	you *sing.* = تو	you *sing.* = تو
him/her = او	him/her = شَ	him/her = او	he/she = او
us = ما	us = مان	us = ما	we = ما
you *pl.* = شما	you *pl.* = تان	you *pl.* = شما	you *pl.* = شما
them = (آنها) ایشان	them = شان	them = (آنها) ایشان	they = (آنها) ایشان

Personal Pronouns (Summary)
(Table 2.2)

Common Reflexive Pronoun & Personal Reflexive Pronouns	Possessive Pronouns		
	Possessive Pronouns (Pronominal Form)	Possessive Pronouns (Adjectival Form)	
		Attached	Detached
خود & خودَم = myself خودَت = yourself خودَش = himself/herself ourselves = خودمان yourselves = خودتان themselves= خودِشان	مالِ من = mine مالِ تو = yours *sing.* مالِ او = his/hers مالِ ما = ours مالِ شما = yours *pl.* theirs = (مالِ آنها) مالِ ایشان	my = مَ your *sing.*= تَ his/her = شَ our = مان your *pl.*= تان their = شان	my = من your *sing.* = تو his/her = او our = ما your *pl.* = شما their = (آنها)ایشان

61

2) Demonstrative Pronouns:
     Some of the most common *"demonstrative pronouns"* are:

❖   این :

/in/

This pronoun refers to a person or an object close to the speaker.

EXAMPLES:

به این نگاه کن!

/be- in- ne.găh- kon/
Look at this!

سارا این را دوست ندارد.

/să.ră- in- ră- dust- na.dă.rad/
 Sara doesn't like this.

❖   آن :

/ăn/

This pronoun refers to a person or an object far from the speaker.

EXAMPLES:

آن را باور نکن!

 /ăn- ră- bă.var- na.kon/
Do not believe that!

من آن را نمی خواهم!

 /man- ăn- ră- ne.mi.ǩă.ham/
I don't want that!

Note:

The plural forms of این /in/ and آن /ăn/ are:

آن ها (آنها) /ăn.hă/ and این ها (اینها) /in.hă/.

EXAMPLES:

اینها زیبا هستند.

/in.hă- zi.bă- has.tand/
These are beautiful.

آنها جوان هستند.

/ăn.hă- ja.văn- has.tand/
<u>They</u> are young.

❖ همین :

/ha.min/
This pronoun refers to a person or an object (with an emphasis) and shows that the person or object is close to the speaker.

EXAMPLES:

من هم همین را می گویم.

/man- ham- ha.min- ră- mi.gu.yam/
I'm saying <u>this very same</u> [thing].

کتابی که می خواهم، همین است.

/ke.tă.bi- ke- mi.kă.ham- ha.min- ast/
<u>This</u> is the book I want.

❖ همان :

/ha.măn/
This refers to a person or an object (with an emphasis) and shows that the person or object is far from the speaker.

EXAMPLES:

پدرت، همان است که من دیدم.

/pe.da.rat- ha.măn- ast- ke- man- di.dam/
Your father is <u>the one</u> I saw.

من هم همان را خوردم!

/man- ham- ha.măn- ră- kor.dam/
I ate <u>that very same</u> [thing]!

Note:

The plural forms of همین /ha.min/ and همان /ha.măn/ are:

همین ها /ha.min.hă/ and همان ها /ha.măn.hă/.

63

EXAMPLES:

همین ها خوبند!

/ha.min.hǎ- ǩu.band/

<u>These</u> are fine!

اینها، همان هایی است که می خواستم.

/in.hǎ- ha.mǎn.hǎ.yi- ast- ke- mi.ǩǎs.tam/

These are <u>the ones</u> [I] wanted!

3) Indefinite Pronouns:

This group of pronouns represents the general concept of a person or object. The most common *indefinite pronouns* are:

❖ **همه**

/ha.me/

EXAMPLE:

همه خوبند.

/ha.me- ǩu.band/

<u>All</u> is well.

❖ **کسی**

/ka.si/

EXAMPLE:

کسی دارد در می زند.

/ka.si- dǎ.rad- dar- mi.za.nad/

<u>Somebody</u> is knocking on the door.

❖ **هیچکس**

/hič.kas/

EXAMPLE:

هیچکس نگاه نکرد!

/hič.kas- ne.gǎh- na.kard/

<u>Nobody</u> looked!

❖ **هیچ**

/hič/

EXAMPLE:

هیچ نگفتم!

/hič- na.gof.tam/

[I] said <u>nothing</u>!

4) Interrogative Pronouns:

These are essentially the "question words". The most common *interrogative pronouns* are:

❖   چطور

/če.tor/

EXAMPLE:

چطور توانستی به من دروغ بگویی؟

/če.tor- ta.vă.nes.ti- be- man- do.ruğ- be.gu.yi/

<u>How</u> could [you] lie to me?

❖   چه

/če/

EXAMPLE:

در دستت چه داری؟

/dar- das.tat- če- dă.ri/

<u>What</u> do [you] have in your hand?

❖   کی

/key/

EXAMPLE:

کی به دیدن ما می آیید؟

/key- be- di.da.ne- mă- mi.ă.yid/

<u>When</u> do [you] come to see us?

❖   کدام

/ko.dăm/

EXAMPLE:

کدام را دوست داری؟

/ko.dăm- ră- dust- dă.ri/
<u>Which</u> [one] do [you] like?

❖ کجا

/ko.jă/

EXAMPLE:

کجا داری می روی؟

/ko.jă- dă.ri- mi.ra.vi/
<u>Where</u> are [you] going?

❖ که

/ke/

EXAMPLES:

که آنجا خوابیده است؟

/ke- ăn.jă- kă.bi.de- ast/
<u>Who</u> is sleeping there?

که را بوسیدی؟

/ke- ră- bu.si.di/
<u>Whom</u> did [you] kiss?

Note:

If the *question words* are used alone, they are considered *interrogative pronouns* and if they are followed by a noun they will be *interrogative adjectives*.

EXAMPLE:

از چه راهی این شغل را پیدا کردی؟

/az- če- ră.hi- in- šoğl- ră- pey.dă- kar.di/
Through <u>which channel</u> did you find this job?

66

Chapter 2 - Vocabulary

آ

apartment	آپارتمان
wish/dream	آرزو
to prepare	آماده کردن
to come	آمدن
that	آن
there	آنجا
They/them/those	آنها (آن ها)
to sing	آواز خواندن

ا

from	از
to lose	از دست دادن
from the distance	از دور
tear	اشک
to fall	افتادن
but	امّا
exam/test	امتحان
he/she/him/her	او
idea	ایده
they/them	ایشان
here	اینجا
this	این
these	اینها (این ها)

ب

with respect	با احترام
carefully	با احتیاط
happily	با خوشحالی
time	بار
to open	باز کردن
to believe	باور کردن
to come true	بر آورده شدن
for	برایِ
to pick up	برداشتن
to take	بردن
to return	برگشتن
to kiss	بوسیدن
to	به
hardly	به سختی
better	بهتر
more	بیشتر

پ

park	پارک
father	پدر
to ask	پرسیدن
to wear	پوشیدن
to find	پیدا کردن

ت

you *sing.*	تو

to be able to/ can	توانستن

ج

road	جادّه
present	جایزه
to answer	جواب دادن
young	جوان

چ

how?	چطور؟
several	چندین
what?	چه؟
what is?	چیست؟

ح

to solve	حل کردن

خ

house/home	خانه
to be ashamed/ to be shy	خجالت کشیدن
to dry	خشک کردن
to sleep	خوابیدن
to want	خواستن
sister	خواهر
good/well	خوب
yourself	خودت
yourselves	خودتان
himself/herself	خودش

themselves	خودشان
myself	خودم
ourselves	خودمان
to eat	خوردن
sweetest	خوش ترین
street	خیابان
wet	خیس
very	خیلی

د

to give	دادن
to have	داشتن
girl/daughter	دختر
in/door	در
to hug	در آغوش کشیدن
about	درباره ی
to knock on the door	در زدن
in the midst of	در میانِ
to lie	دروغ گفتن
hand	دست
to invite	دعوت کردن
far	دور
friend	دوست
to like/ to love	دوست داشتن
second	دوّم
to see	دیدن
yesterday	دیروز

ر

restaurant	رستوران
to go	رفتن
to dance	رقصیدن
boss	رئیس

ز

to live	زندگی کردن
beautiful	زیبا

س

trip	سفر
dog	سگ
heavy	سنگین
apple	سیب

ش

job	شغل
to break	شکستن
you *pl.*	شما
to know/to recognize	شناختن
husband	شوهر

ص

to call on	صدا کردن

ض

pronoun	ضمیر

ط

floor	طبقه

ع

to cross	عبور کردن

غ

food	غذا
to feed	غذا دادن

ف

tomorrow	فردا
to send	فرستادن

ق

old	قدیمی
red	قرمز

ک

work	کار
computer	کامپیوتر
book	کتاب
which?	کدام؟
somebody	کسی
country	کشور
shoe	کفش
to help	کمک کردن
who?/whom?	که؟

PRONOUNS

when?	کِی؟
bag	کیف

گ

to tell	گفتن
flowerpot	گلدان

ل

clothes	لباس
smile	لبخند
to smile	لبخند زدن

م

we/us	ما
mother	مادر
car	ماشین
theirs	مال آنها
his/hers	مالِ او
theirs	مالِ ایشان
yours sing.	مالِ تو
yours pl.	مالِ شما
mine	مالِ من
school	مدرسه
manager	مدیر
problem/ difficult	مشکل
I/me	من
hair	مو

ن

letter	نامه
to show	نشان دادن
to look	نگاه کردن
new	نو
newer	نوتر
to write	نوشتن
New York	نیویورک

ه

the same/that/ that very	همان
everybody/all	همه
the same/this/ this very	همین
nothing	هیچ
nobody	هیچکس

ی

to teach	یاد دادن

Test Yourself:

2.1 Rewrite the sentences below by changing the underlined nouns or noun phrases into the appropriate **personal pronouns (as subjects).**

Example:

۱ – <u>الیزابت</u> دیروز از سفر برگشت.

/e.li.ză.bet- di.ruz- az- sa.far- bar.gašt/
Elizabeth returned from the trip yesterday.

او دیروز از سفر برگشت.

۲– <u>من و دوستانم</u> به پارک می رویم.

/man- va- dus.tă.nam- be- părk- mi.ra.vim/
My friends and I go to the park.

۳– <u>سینا و پدرش</u> به دیدنِ من آمدند.

/si.nă- va- pe.da.raš- be- di.da.ne- man- ă.ma.dand/
Sina and his father came to see me.

۴– <u>خواهرم</u> ، دختر خیلی زیبایی ست.

/kă.ha.ram- dok.ta.re- key.li- zi.bă.yist/
My sister is a very beautiful girl.

۵– <u>تو و برادرهایت</u> جوان هستید.

/to- va- ba.ră.dar.hă.yat- ja.văn- has.tid/
You and your brothers are young.

2.2 Rewrite the following sentences, changing the nouns or pronouns shown in the parentheses into **detached personal pronouns (as direct objects)**.

Example: ۱ – سینا (پدر و مادرش) را به سفر می بَرَد.

/si.nă- pe.dar- va- mă.da.raš- ră- be- sa.far- mi.ba.rad/
Sina takes (his father and mother) on a trip.

سینا آنها را به سفر می بَرَد.

۲– من (سارا) را خیلی دوست دارم.

/man- să.ră- ră- key.li- dust- dă.ram/
I love (Sara) very much.

۳- مادرم (من و دوستم) را در رستوران دید.

/mă.da.ram- man- va- dus.tam- ră- dar- res.tu.răn- did/
My mother saw (me and my friend) in the restaurant.

۴- من (تو و دوستانت) را به خانه ام دعوت کردم.

/man- to- va- dus.tă.nat- ră- be- kă.ne.am- daˁ.vat- kar.dam/
I invited (you and your friends) to my house.

۵- الیزابت (دوستم) را به پارک بُرد.

/e.li.ză.bet- dus.tam- ră- be- părk- bord/
Elizabeth took (my friend) to the park.

۶- فردا (مادرم و دوستانش) را به سفر خواهم بُرد.

/far.dă- mă.da.ram- va- dus.tă.naš- ră- be- sa.far- kă.ham- bord/
I will take (my mother and her friends) on a trip tomorrow.

۷- ما (دخترمان) را به لندن فرستادیم.

/mă- dok̆.ta.re.măn- ră- be- lan.dan- fe.res.tă.dim/
We sent (our daughter) to London.

۸- سینا دارد (دوستش) را می بوسد.

/si.nă- dă.rad- dus.taš- ră- mi.bu.sad/
Sina is kissing (his friend).

2.3 Rewrite the following sentences, changing the underlined **attached personal pronouns (as direct objects)** into **detached personal pronouns (as direct objects)**.

Example:

۱- من دیروز در پارک دیدمَت .

/man- di.ruz- dar- părk- di.da.mat/
I saw you in the park yesterday.

من دیروز تو را در پارک دیدم.

۲- ما به سختی شناختیمشان.

/mă- be- sak̆.ti- še.nak̆.ti.me.šăn/
We hardly recognized them.

74

۳- پدرش با خوشحالی بوسیدَش.

/pe.da.raš- bǎ- ǩoš.hǎ.li- bu.si.daš/

His/Her father kissed <u>him/her</u> happily.

۴- سارا دوستَم دارد.

/sǎ.rǎ- dus.tam- dǎ.rad/

Sara loves <u>me</u>.

۵- مادر سینا از پارک به خانه آوردمان.

/mǎ.da.re- si.nǎ- az- pǎrk- be- ǩǎ.ne- ǎ.var.de.mǎn/

Sina's mother brought <u>us</u> home from park.

۶- صدا کردَمَش.

/se.dǎ- kar.da.maš/

[I] called on <u>her/him</u>.

۷- سینا در آغوشَم کشید.

/si.nǎ- dar- ǎ.ǧu.šam- ke.šid/

Sina hugged <u>me</u>.

۸– مَن برای اِمتحان آماده <u>شان</u> کردَم.

/man- ba.ră.ye- em.te.hăn- ă.mă.de.šăn- kar.dam/
I prepared <u>them</u> for the exam.

2.4 Rewrite the following sentences, by changing the underlined **attached personal pronouns (as indirect objects)** into the **detached personal pronouns (as indirect objects)** as indicated in the parentheses. To facilitate the process, you may first separate the **attached personal pronouns (as indirect objects)** from the verbs. Keep in mind that you need to use the preposition به /be/ before the **detached personal pronouns (as indirect objects)**.

Example:

۱– گُفتَ<u>مَت</u>: « بیا ! » (تو)

/gof.ta.mat- bi.yă/
I told <u>you</u>: come!

گُفتَم + َت = « بیا ! »

به تو گُفتم: « بیا ! »

۲– با خوشحالی غذا دادَ<u>مَش</u>. (او)

/bă- ǩoš.hă.li- ǧa.ză- dă.da.maš/
I fed <u>him/her</u> happily.

۳- فارسی را یادتان دادَم. (شما)

/făr.si- ră- yă.de.tăn- dă.dam/

[I] taught <u>you</u> Persian.

_____

_____

۴- با احترام جوابَت دادَم. (تو)

/bă- eh.te.răm- ja.vă.bat- dă.dam/

[I] answered <u>you</u> with respect.

_____

_____

۵- خانه را نشان دادَمشان. (آنها)

/kă.ne- ră- ne.šăn- dă.da.me.šăn/

[I] showed <u>them</u> the house.

_____

_____

۶- با شوق نگاهَش کَردم. (او)

/bă- šoğ- ne.gă.haš- kar.dam/

[I] looked at <u>her/him</u> with joy.

_____

_____

2.5 Rewrite the following sentences, changing the personal possessive nouns, possessive pronouns and noun phrases shown in the parentheses into **detached personal possessive pronouns.**

Example:

۱- کیفِ (سارا) قرمز است.

/ki.fe- să.ră- ğer.mez- ast/

Sara's bag is red.

کیفِ او قرمز است.

۲- ماشینِ (پدر و مادرم) خیلی قدیمی است.

/mă.ši.ne- pe.dar- va- mă.da.ram- ǩey.li- ğa.di.mi- ast/

My mother and father's car is very old.

۳- کفش هایِ (تو و الیزابت) زیبا هستند.

/kafš.hă.ye- to- va- e.li.ză.bet- zi.bă - has.tand/

Elizabeth's and your shoes are beautiful.

۴- سارا، دوستِ (من و خواهرم) است.

/să.ră- dus.te- man- va- ǩă.ha.ram- ast/

Sara is my sister's and my friend.

۵– کتاب های (سارا و سینا) سنگین هستند.

/ke.tăb.hă.ye- să.ră- va- si.nă- san.gin- has.tand/

Sara's and Sina's books are heavy.

۶– دست های (تو و سام و الیزابت) خیس هستند.

/dast.hă.ye- to- va- săm- va- e.li.ză.bet- ǩis- has.tand/

Sam's and Elizabeth's and your hands are wet.

۷– مدرسه ی (من و خواهرهایم) از اینجا خیلی دور است.

/mad.re.se.ye- man- va- ǩă.har.hă.yam- az- in.jă- ǩey.li- dur- ast/

My sisters' and my school is very far from here.

۸– آپارتمانِ (شوهرم) در طبقه ی دوّم است.

/ă.păr.te.mă.ne- šo.ha.ram- dar- ta.ba.ǧe.ye- dov.vom- ast/

My husband's apartment is on the second floor.

2.6 Rewrite the following sentences, by changing the underlined **detached personal possessive pronouns** into **attached personal possessive pronouns**.

Example:

۱– من می خواهم با خواهرِ تو برقصم.

/man- mi.ǩă.ham- bă- ǩă.ha.re- to- be.raǧ.sam/

I want to dance with your sister.

من می خواهم با خواهرَت برقصم.

۲- ما کشور شما را دوست داریم.

/mă- keš.va.re- šo.mă- ră- dust- dă.rim/

We like your country.

۳- تو کیف من را گم کردی.

/to- ki.fe- man- ră- gom- kar.di/

You lost my bag.

۴- دخترهای ما در لندن زندگی می کنند.

/dok.tar.hă.ye- mă- dar- lan.dan- zen.de.gi- mi.ko.nand/

Our daughters live in London.

۵- گلدان من افتاد و شکست.

/gol.dă.ne- man- of.tăd- va- še.kast/

My flowerpot fell and broke.

۶- ماشین های آنها نو هستند.

/mă.šin.hă.ye- ăn.hă- no- has.tand/

Their cars are new.

80

۷- سگ او خیلی می خوابد.

/sa.ge- u- ǩey.li- mi.ǩǎ.bad/

His/Her dog sleeps a lot.

۸- دوستان شما دوست دارند آواز بخوانند.

/dus.tǎ.ne- šo.mǎ- dust- dǎ.rand- ǎ.vǎz- be.ǩǎ.nand/

Your friends like to sing.

2.7 Rewrite the following sentences by changing the pronouns in the parentheses into the appropriate **reflexive pronouns.**

Example:

۱- من دوست دارم درباره ی (من) بنویسم.

/man- dust- dǎ.ram- dar.bǎ.re.ye- (man)- be.ne.vi.sam/

I like to write about myself.

من دوست دارم درباره ی خودَم بنویسم.

۲- آنها باید این مشکل را (آنها) حل کنند.

/ǎn.hǎ- bǎ.yad- in- moš.kel- rǎ- (ǎn.hǎ)- hal- ko.nand/

They have to solve this problem themselves.

81

۳- تو باید از (تو) بپرسی که کدام شغل را بیشتر دوست داری.

/to- bă.yad- az- (to)- be.por.si- ke- ko.dăm- šoğl- ră- biš.tar- dust- dă.ri/
You should ask yourself which job you like better.

۴- شما باید از (شما) خجالت بکشید!

/šo.mă- bă.yad- az- (šo.mă)- ǩe.jă.lat- be.ke.šid/
You must be ashamed of yourselves!

۵- ما می توانیم به (ما) کمک کنیم.

/mă- mi.ta.vă.nim- be- (mă)- ko.mak- ko.nim/
We can help ourselves.

۶- او بهتر از هر کسی (او) را می شناسد.

/u- beh.tar- az- har- ka.si- (u)- ră- mi.še.nă.sad/
He/She knows himself/herself better than anybody.

2.8 Complete the following sentences by writing the **pronominal form** of the **personal possessive pronouns** for the words shown in parentheses.

Example:

۱ – این (سیبِ من) است.

/in- si.be- man- ast/
(This is my apple.)

این سیب،   مالِ من   ‫_____‬   است.

/in- sib- ...... - ast/
(This apple is mine.)

۲- این ماشین قرمز، (ماشین ما) است.

/in- mǎ.ši.ne- ğer.mez- mǎ.ši.ne- mǎ- ast/
(This red car is our car.)

این ماشینِ قرمز، ‫_____‬ است.

/in-mǎ.ši.ne- ğer.mez- ...... -ast/
(This red car is ours.)

۳- من (کتابِ تو) را برداشتم.

/man- ke.tǎ.be- to- rǎ- bar.dǎš.tam/
(I picked up your books.)

من ‫_____‬ را برداشتم.

/man- ...... - rǎ- bar.dǎš.tam/
(I picked up yours.)

۴- تو (غذای او) را خوردی.

/to- ğa.zǎ.ye- u- rǎ- ǩor.di/
(You ate his/her food.)

تو ‫_____‬ را خوردی.

/to- ...... - rǎ- ǩor.di/
(You ate his/hers.)

83

۵- (خانه ی شما) از (خانه ی آنها) نوتر است.

/kǎ.ne.ye- šo.ma- az- kǎ.ne.ye- ǎn.hǎ- no.tar- ast/
(Your house is newer than their house.)

_____ از _____ نو تر است.

/...... az- ...... no.tar- ast/
(Yours is newer than theirs.)

۶- مریم (لباس های تو) را پوشیده است.

/mar.yam- le.bǎs.hǎ.ye- to- rǎ- pu.ši.de- ast/
(Maryam is wearing your clothes.)

مریم _____ را پوشیده است.

/mar.yam- ...... - rǎ- pu.ši.de- ast/
(Maryam is wearing yours.)

۷- (کامپیوتر من) بهتر از (کامپیوتر تو) است.

/kǎm.pi.yu.te.re- man- beh.tar- az- kǎm.pi.yu.te.re- to- ast/
(My computer is better than your computer.)

_____ بهتر از _____ است.

/ .... beh.tar- az- .... – ast/
(Mine is better than yours.)

۸- این کلید، (کلیدِ من) نیست.

/in- ke.lid- ke.li.de- man- nist/
(This key is not my key.)

این کلید، _____ نیست.

/in- ke.lid- ......- nist/
(This key is not mine.)

84

۹- کیفی که پیدا کردی، (کیفِ ما) بود.

/ki.fi- ke- pey.dă- kar.di- ki.fe- mă- bud/

(The bag you found was our bag.)

کیفی که پیدا کردی، _____ بود.

/ki.fi- ke- pey.dă- kar.di- ....- bud/

(The bag you found was ours.)

CHAPTER 3

ADJECTIVES

صفَت ها

‎َ‎
/se.fat.hă/

An adjective is a word that describes a noun. There are different kinds of adjectives. They are generally classified as either *"simple adjectives"* or *"compound adjectives"* based on their structures.

- Simple Adjectives:

    These adjectives take the form of one word.

    EXAMPLES:

    big   /bo.zorg/   بزرگ

    red   /ğer.mez/   قرمز

- Compound Adjectives:

These adjectives are combinations of more than one element, and may include a noun, an adjective, a preposition, a prefix or a suffix.

EXAMPLES:

worthless   /bi.ar.zeš/   بی ارزش = بی + ارزش

good-hearted   /ǩoš.ǧalb/   خوش قلب = خوش + قلب

Adjectives may also be divided into the nine following groups based on their meanings and functions within sentences:

1) Descriptive Adjectives   2) Demonstrative Adjectives
3) Adjectives of Numbers   4) Adjectives of Competence
5) Indefinite Adjectives   6) Comparative Forms of Adjectives
7) Superlative Forms of Adjectives   8) Interrogative Adjectives   9) Positive and Negative Adjectives

1) Descriptive Adjectives:

These adjectives describe a noun's size, shape, color, amount or texture. They also show the origin, the relation and the condition of a noun. They come after nouns, and they are used in singular form with both singular and plural nouns. *"Descriptive adjectives"* are divided into three groups:

a) Adjectives of Relation
b) Adjectives derived from the Present Stem of a Verb
c) Adjectives derived from the Past Stem of a Verb

a) *Adjectives of Relation:*
- These adjectives are attributed to a place, a person, an object or a meaning and they are formed by adding one of the following five suffixes to the end of a noun or sometimes to the end of another adjective:

ی - /i/

ین - /in/

انه - /ǎ.ne/

انی - /ǎ.ni/

گانه - /gǎ.ne/

87

❖ ی : ❖
/i/

EXAMPLES:

Iranian   /i.rǎ.ni/   ایرانی = ی + ایران

English/British   /en.ge.li.si/   انگلیسی = ی + انگلیس

celestial   /ǎ.se.mǎ.ni/   آسمانی = ی + آسمان

urban   /šah.ri/   شهری = ی + شهر

sunny   /ǎf.tǎ.bi/   آفتابی = ی + آفتاب

Note:

If the noun ends in ا /ǎ/, the suffix ی /i/ converts into یی /yi/.

EXAMPLES:

Asian   /ǎ.si.yǎ.yi/   آسیایی

African   /ǎf.ri.ğǎ.yi/   آفریقایی

American   /ǎm.ri.kǎ.yi/   آمریکایی

Note:

If the noun ends in ه — ـه with the /e/ sound, the suffix ی /i/ changes into

ای /i/ .

EXAMPLES:

periodic/periodical   /do.re.i/   دوره ای = ای + دوره

rocky   /sǎk.re.i/   صخره ای = ای + صخره

silvery/silver tone   /noğ.re.i/   نقره ای

88

Note:

On some occasions, when the noun ends in ه — ـه with the /e/ sound, ه — ـه changes into گ /g/.

EXAMPLES:

domestic   /kǎ.ne.gi/   خانه◄   خانگ   +   ی   =   خانگی

weekly   /haf.te.gi/   هفته◄   هفتگ   +   ی   =   هفتگی

❖ **ین** :
    /in/

EXAMPLES:

ancient   /pi.šin/   پیش + ین = پیشین

colorful   /ran.gin/   رنگ + ین = رنگین

golden   /zar.rin/   زرّ + ین = زرّین

❖ **انه** :
    /ǎ.ne/

EXAMPLES:

daily   /ru.zǎ.ne/   روز + انه = روزانه

feminine   /za.nǎ.ne/   زن + انه = زنانه

respectful   /moh.ta.ra.mǎ.ne/   مُحترم + انه = مُحترمانه

❖ **انی** :
    /ǎ.ni/

EXAMPLES:

physical   /jes.mǎ.ni/   جسم + انی = جسمانی

luminous   /nu.ră.ni/   نور + انی = نورانی

lengthy   /tu.lă.ni/   طول + انی = طولانی

❖   گانه :

/gă.ne/

EXAMPLES:

bi-   /do.gă.ne/   دو + گانه = دوگانه

multi-   /čand.gă.ne/   چند + گانه = چندگانه

separate   /jo.dă.gă.ne/   جدا + گانه = جداگانه

b) *Adjectives derived from the present stem of a verb:*

- These adjectives are formed by adding one of the following three suffixes to the end of the present stem of the verb:

- نَده   /an.de/

- ان   /ăn/

- ا   /ă/

❖   نَده :

/an.de/

EXAMPLES:

receptive   /gi.ran.de/   گیر + نده = گیرنده

generous/giving   /bak̆.šan.de/   بخش + نده = بخشنده

fragile   /še.ka.nan.de/   شکن + نده = شکننده

❖   ان :

/ăn/

90

EXAMPLES:

shining /tă.băn/   تاب + ان = تابان

crying /ger.yăn/   گری + ان = گریان

shaking /lar.zăn/   لرز + ان = لرزان

:   ا ❖

/ă/

EXAMPLES:

legible /ḱă.nă/   خوان + ا = خوانا

knowledgeable /dă.nă/   دان + ا = دانا

talking /gu.yă/   گوی + ا = گویا

c) *Adjectives derived from the past stem of a verb:*

- These adjectives are formed by adding the suffix ه — ﻪ with the /e/ sound to the end of the past stem.

EXAMPLES:

eaten /ḱor.de/   خورد + ه = خورده

polluted /ă.lu.de/   آلود + ه = آلوده

broken /še.kas.te/   شکست + ه = شکسته

Note:

Adjectives derived from the past stem of a verb are also called *"objective adjectives"* and are equivalent to the *past participle* in English language.

Note:

The noun always connects to its adjective with the vowel ____ /e/ *(kasre-ye ezăfe).*

91

broken heart   /ğal.be- še.kas.te/   قلب شکسته = قلبِ شکسته = شکسته + قلب

feminine clothes   /le.bǎ.se- za.nǎ.ne/   لباس زنانه = لباسِ زنانه = زنانه + لباس

Note:

If the noun ends in any of the following three letters, the vowel ___ /e/ *(kasre-ye*

ezǎfe) changes into   ی   /ye/:

- ا   /ǎ/

- و   /u/

- ه — ـه   /e/

EXAMPLES:

beautiful world   /don.yǎ.ye- zi.bǎ/   دنیای زیبا = دنیای زیبا = زیبا + دنیا

long hair   /mu.ye- bo.land/   موی بلند = موی بلند = بلند + مو

small house   /ǩǎ.ne.ye- ku.čak/   خانه‌ی کوچک = خانه‌ی کوچک = کوچک + خانه

2) Demonstrative Adjectives:

Some of the most common *demonstrative adjectives* are:

❖   این :

/in/

This adjective defines a *singular* or *plural noun* (person or object) and shows that the noun is close to the speaker.

EXAMPLES:
- for *singular nouns*:

<u>this</u> house   /in- ǩǎ.ne/   این خانه

<u>this</u> woman   /in- zan/   این زن

- for *plural nouns*:

these houses   /in- kǎ.ne.hǎ/   این خانه ها

these women   /in- zan.hǎ/   این زن ها

❖ آن :   آن
  /ǎn/

This adjective defines a *singular* or *plural noun* (person or object) and shows that the noun is far from the speaker.

EXAMPLES:

- for *singular nouns*:

that school   /ǎn- mad.re.se/   آن مدرسه

that man   /ǎn- mard/   آن مرد

- for *plural nouns*:

those schools   /ǎn- mad.re.se.hǎ/   آن مدرسه ها

those men   /ǎn- mard.hǎ/   آن مرد ها

❖ همین :   همین
  /ha.min/

This adjective defines a *singular* or *plural noun* (person or object) with an emphasis and shows that the noun is close to the speaker.

EXAMPLES:

- for *singular nouns*:

من هم همین احساس را دارم !

/man- ham- ha.min- eh.sǎs- rǎ- dǎ.ram/
I have the same feeling, too!

- for *plural nouns*:

من به همین مشکلات اشاره کردم.

/man- be- ha.min- moš.ke.lǎt- e.šǎ.re- kar.dam/
I mentioned the same issues.

همان : ❖

/ha.mǎn/

This adjective defines a *singular* or *plural noun* (person or object) with an emphasis and shows that the noun is far from the speaker.

EXAMPLES:

- for *singular nouns*:

من هم همان همبرگر را خوردم.

/man- ham- ha.mǎn- ham.ber.ger- rǎ- ǩor.dam/
I ate <u>that very same</u> burger.

- for *plural nouns*:

آن خانه ها، همان خانه هایی هستند که برایت گفتم.

/ǎn- ǩǎ.ne.hǎ- ha.mǎn- ǩǎ.ne.hǎ.yi- has.tand- ke- ba.rǎ.yat- gof.tam/
Those houses are <u>the ones</u> that [I] told you about.

3) Adjectives of Number:

There are two types of adjectives in this group:
a) Cardinal Numbers
b) Ordinal Numbers

a) *Cardinal numbers* are used to indicate quantity. As adjectives, they come before the noun.

EXAMPLES:

<u>two</u> chairs /do- san.da.li/ دو صندلی

<u>five</u> girls /panj- doǩ.tar/ پنج دختر

<u>twelve</u> tables /da.vǎz.dah- miz/ دوازده میز

b) *Ordinal numbers* are used to indicate the relative position or order of a noun in relation to other nouns. As adjectives, they come either before the noun or after the noun.

EXAMPLES:
- before the noun:

<u>first</u> job /av.va.lin- šoǧl/ اوّلین شغل

<u>fifth</u> trip /pan.jo.min- sa.far/ پنجمین سفر

<u>twelfth</u> row /da.vǎz.da.ho.min- ra.dif/ دوازدهمین ردیف

- after the noun:

first job   /šoğ.le- av.val/   شغلِ اوّل

fifth trip   /sa.fa.re- pan.jom/   سفرِ پنجم

twelfth row   /ra.di.fe- da.văz.da.hom/   ردیفِ دوازدهم

Note:

Ordinal numbers that come after the noun always get connected to the noun with the

vowel ___ /e/ *(kasre-ye ezăfe)*.

Note:

If the noun ends in any of the following three letters, the vowel ___ /e/ *(kasre-ye*

ezăfe) changes into   ی   /ye/:

- ا   /ă/

- و   /u/

- ه — ٵ   /e/

EXAMPLES:

last sound   /se.dă.ye- ă.ḱar/   صدا + آخر = صدای آخر

first shovel   /pă.ru.ye- av.val/   پارو + اوّل = پاروی اوّل

third floor   /ta.ba.ğe.ye- sev.vom/   طبقه + سوّم = طبقه ی سوّم

4) Adjectives of Competence:

These adjectives describe a quality to the worth of a noun. They are formed by
adding the suffix   ی   /i/ to the end of an infinitive.

EXAMPLES:

edible /ǩor.da.ni/ خوردنی = ی + خوردن

loveable/lovely /dust- dǎš.ta.ni/ دوست داشتنی = ی + دوست داشتن

well worth reading /ǩǎn.da.ni/ خواندنی = ی + خواندن

5) Indefinite Adjectives:

These adjectives refer to unspecified nouns. Some come before the noun and some after the noun.

EXAMPLES:
- before the noun:

<u>any</u> time /har- bǎr/ هر بار

<u>few</u> days /čand- ruz/ چند روز

- after the noun:

<u>another</u> day /ru.ze- di.gar/ روزِ دیگر

<u>small</u> amount /meǧ.dǎ.re- an.dak/ مقدارِ اندک

Note:

Adjectives that follow a noun are linked to the noun with the vowel ___ /e/ *(kasre-ye ezǎfe)*.

Keep in Mind: If *indefinite adjectives* are used in isolation, or in the absence of a noun, they become *indefinite pronouns*. An exception to this rule is هر /har/, which cannot be used alone and is always followed by a noun.

6) Comparative forms of Adjectives:

These adjectives express a relative greater or lesser degree of a quality. This type of adjective is formed by adding the suffix تر /tar/ to the end of an adjective.

EXAMPLES:

whiter /se.fid.tar/ سفیدتر = تر + سفید

more beautiful /zi.bǎ.tar/ زیباتر = تر + زیبا

bigger /bo.zorg.tar/ بزرگ تر = تر + بزرگ

Comparative forms of adjectives are usually used with the preposition از /az/ which is the equivalent to "than" in English language.

Comparative forms of adjectives may take one of two different forms in a sentence. The meaning is not affected by the form.

EXAMPLES:

آپارتمان من بزرگ تر از آپارتمان توست.

/ă.păr.te.mă.ne- man- bo.zorg.tar- az- ă.păr.te.mă.ne- tost/
My apartment is bigger <u>than</u> your apartment.

آپارتمان من از آپارتمان تو بزرگ تر است.

/ă.păr.te.mă.ne- man- az- ă.păr.te.mă.ne- to- bo.zorg.tar- ast/
My apartment is bigger <u>than</u> your apartment.

7) Superlative forms of Adjectives:

These adjectives express the greatest or the least amount or intensity of a quality found among all subjects compared. They are formed by adding the suffix ترین /ta.rin/ to the end of an adjective.

EXAMPLES:

whitest   /se.fid.ta.rin/ سفیدترین = ترین + سفید

most beautiful   /zi.bă.ta.rin/ زیباترین = ترین + زیبا

biggest   /bo.zorg.ta.rin/ بزرگ ترین = ترین + بزرگ

Superlative forms of adjectives may be used in the sentence in two forms: one is more common and the other is less common. The meaning is the same in both forms.

EXAMPLES:
- more common form:

من خوشبخت ترین زن دنیا هستم.

/man- ḱoš.baḱt.ta.rin- za.ne- don.yă- has.tam/
I am the happiest woman in the world.

- less common form:

من خوشبخت ترین زن های دنیا هستم.

/man- ḱoš.baḱt.ta.ri.ne- zan.hă.ye- don.yă- has.tam/
I am the happiest of all women in the world.

Note:

The *comparative* and *superlative forms of the adjective* "good" are irregular:

good   /ǩub/ خوب

better   /beh.tar/ بهتر

best   /beh.ta.rin/ بهترین

8) Interrogative Adjectives:

These are essentially the "question words". *Interrogative adjectives* are question words used with a noun.

EXAMPLES:

چه روزی آزاد هستید؟

/če- ru.zi- ǎ.zǎd- has.tid/
<u>What</u> day are [you] free?

کدام رستوران را بیشتر دوست دارید؟

/ko.dǎm- res.tu.rǎn- rǎ- biš.tar- dust- dǎ.rid/
<u>Which</u> restaurant do [you] like better?

چند بار به ایران سفر کرده ای؟

/čand- bǎr- be- i.rǎn- sa.far- kar.de.i/
<u>How many</u> times have [you] traveled to Iran?

Keep in Mind: If question words are used alone, they are classified as *interrogative pronouns.*

9) Positive and Negative Adjectives:

❖ *Positive adjectives* are usually formed by adding the preposition با /bǎ/ to the beginning of a noun.

EXAMPLES:

smart   /bǎ.huš/ باهوش = هوش + با

patient /bǎ.ho.se.le/ با حوصله = حوصله + با

98

faithful   /bă.i.măn/   با + ایمان = با ایمان

> ❖ *Negative adjectives* are usually formed by adding the preposition بی /bi/ to the beginning of a noun.

EXAMPLES:

shameless   /bi.šarm/   بی + شرم = بی شرم

loveless   /bi.mo.hab.bat/   بی + محبّت = بی محبّت

careless   /bi.değ.ğat/   بی + دقّت = بی دقّت

> - *Negative adjectives* may also be formed by adding the prefix نا /nă/ to the beginning of another adjective or to the present stem of a verb:

EXAMPLES:
- prefix نا + adjective:

unfamiliar   /nă.ă.še.nă/   نا + آشنا = ناآشنا

impure   /nă.păk/   نا + پاک = ناپاک

EXAMPLES:
- prefix نا + present stem of verb:

ignorant   /nă.dăn/   نا + دان (دانستن) = نادان

hard-to-find   /nă.yăb/   نا + یاب (یافتن) = نایاب

Chapter 3 – Vocabulary

Iranian	ایرانی
this	این

آ

apartment	آپارتمان
last	آخر
quiet	آرام
free	آزاد
celestial	آسمانی
Asian	آسیایی
sunny	آفتابی
African	آفریقایی
Germany	آلمان
to pollute	آلودن
polluted	آلوده
American	آمریکایی
that	آن

ا

feeling	احساس
European	اروپایی
to mention/ to point out	اشاره کردن
small	اندک
English/British	انگلیسی
first	اوّل
first	اوّلین
Italy	ایتالیا
Iran	ایران

ب

faithful	با ایمان
patient	با حوصله
believable	باورکردنی
unbelievable	باورنکردنی
smart	باهوش
generous/giving	بخشنده
bad	بد
snow	برف
big	بزرگ
to close	بستن
very	بسیار
long/tall	بلند
better	بهتر
best	بهترین
worthless	بی ارزش
more	بیشتر
shameless	بی شرم
careless	بی دقّت
loveless	بی محبّت

پ

shovel	پارو
to cook	پختن

adorable	پرستیدنی
five	پنج
fifth	پنجم
fifth	پنجمین
old	پیر
ancient	پیشین

ت

shining	تابان
to shine	تابیدن
to fear	ترسیدن

ج

separate	جداگانه
physical	جسمانی

چ

How many?	چند؟
a few days	چند روز
multi-	چندگانه
What?	چه؟

خ

domestic	خانگی
house/home	خانه
to laugh	خندیدن
desirable	خواستنی
legible	خوانا

well worth reading	خواندنی
to eat	خوردن
edible	خوردنی
eaten	خورده
good	خوب
happiest	خوشبخت ترین
good-hearted	خوش قلب

د

to have	داشتن
knowledgeable	دانا
girl/daughter	دختر
tree	درخت
world	دنیا
two	دو
twelve	دوازده
twelfth	دوازدهم
twelfth	دوازدهمین
fiend	دوست
to like/to love	دوست داشتن
lovable/lovely	دوست داشتنی
disposable	دور انداختنی
periodic/periodical	دوره ای
bi-	دوگانه
to see	دیدن
eye-catching	دیدنی

ر

row	ردیف
restaurant	رستوران
to go	رفتن
color	رنگ
colorful	رنگین
day	روز
daily	روزانه
another day	روز دیگر

ز

language/tongue	زبان
golden	زرّین
woman/wife	زن
feminine	زنانه
beautiful	زیبا

س

easy/simple	ساده
hard	سخت
cold	سرد
trip	سفر
to travel	سفر کردن
white	سفید
third	سوّم
black	سیاه

ش

branch	شاخه
happy	شاد
job	شغل
to break	شکستن
broken	شکسته
fragile	شکننده
to hear	شنیدن
worth listening to	شنیدنی
husband	شوهر
urban	شهری

ص

rocky	صخره ای
sound	صدا
adjective	صفت
chair	صندلی

ط

floor	طبقه
lengthy/long	طولانی

ع

exchangeable	عوض کردنی

ق

red	قرمز

ک

Canada	کانادا
book	کتاب
Which?	کدام؟
to do	کردن
country	کشور
short	کوتاه
small/little	کوچک
alley	کوچه

گ

warm	گرم
crying	گریان
to tell/to say	گفتن
worth mentioning	گفتنی
talking	گویا
receptive	گیرنده

ل

clothes	لباس
shaky	لرزان
to shake	لرزیدن
to limp	لنگیدن

م

to stay	ماندن
enduring	ماندنی

respectful	محترمانه
school	مدرسه
man	مرد
mortal	مردنی
issue/difficult	مشکل
amount	مقدار
Mexico	مکزیک
hair	مو
hospitable	مهمان نواز
table/desk	میز

ن

restless	نا آرام
unfamiliar	نا آشنا
blind	نابینا
impure	ناپاک
ignorant	نادان
to moan	نالیدن
hard-to-find	نایاب
soft	نرم
silvery/silver tone	نقره ای
	نورانی

ه

any time	هربار
weekly	هفتگی

ADJECTIVES

same/that/that very	همان
hamburger	همبرگر
same/this/this very	همین

ی

to learn	یاد گرفتن

Test Yourself:

3.1 Look at the words below. Find the **compound adjectives** in the list and break them into their constituent elements such as: adjectives, nouns, prepositions, prefixes, suffixes. Then write the elements in the spaces provided. There are 10 **compound adjectives** in this exercise.

warm /garm/ گرم

short /ku.tăh/ کوتاه

good-hearted /ǩoš.ǧalb/ خوش قلب

smart /bă.huš/ باهوش

loveable/lovely /dust- dăš.ta.ni/ دوست داشتنی

bad /bad/ بد

shameless /bi.šarm/ بی شرم

generous/giving /bаǩ.šan.de/ بخشنده

ADJECTIVES

soft /narm/ نرم

hard /sakt/ سخت

restless /nă.ă.răm/ نا آرام

hospitable /meh.măn.na.văz/ مهمان نواز

worthless /bi.ar.zeš/ بی ارزش

cold /sard/ سرد

old /pir/ پیر

sunny /ăf.tă.bi/ آفتابی

believable /bă.var- kar.da.ni/ باور کردنی

Example :	قلب ‎ + ‎ خوش	۱-

۲- _____ + _____

۳- _____ + _____ + _____

106

_____ + _____ ۴-

_____ + _____ ۵-

_____ + _____ ۶-

_____ + _____ ۷-

_____ + _____ ۸-

_____ + _____ ۹-

_____ + _____ + _____ ۱۰-

3.2 Form **adjectives of competence** from these **infinitives** by adding the suffix ی /i/ .

ا – دوست داشتن /dust- dǎš.tan/ (to like/to love)   **Example:**

(lovable/lovely) دوست داشتنی = ی + داشتن + دوست

۲- خوردن /ḱor.dan/ (to eat)

(edible) _____ = _____ + _____

۳- دیدن /di.dan/ (to see)

(eye-catching) _____ = _____ + _____

۴- خواندن /ḱăn.dan/ (to read)

(well worth reading) _____ = _____ + _____

۵- شنیدن /še.ni.dan/ (to hear)

(worth listening to) _____ = _____ + _____

۶- باور کردن /bă.var- kar.dan/ (to believe)

(believable) _____ = _____ + _____ + _____

7- باور نکردن /bă.var- na.kar.dan/ (not to believe)

(unbelievable) _____ = _____ + _____ + _____

8- ماندن /măn.dan/ (to stay)

(enduring) _____ = _____ + _____

9- پرستیدن /pa.ras.ti.dan/ (to adore)

(adorable) _____ = _____ + _____

10 - شکستن /še.kas.tan/ (to break)

(fragile) _____ = _____ + _____

11- مردن /mor.dan/ (to die)

(mortal) _____ = _____ + _____

12 - گفتن /gof.tan/ (to tell)

(worth mentioning) _____ = _____ + _____

ADJECTIVES

۱۳ – خواستن /kǎs.tan/ (to want)

(desirable) _____ = _____ + _____

۱۴ – عوض کردن /ʻa.vaz- kar.dan/ (to change)

(exchangeable) _____ = _____ + _____ + _____

۱۵ – دور انداختن /dur- an.dǎk.tan/ (to throw away)

(disposable) _____ = _____ + _____ + _____

3.3 Turn the following **verbs** into **adjectives** by adding the suffix ان /ǎn/ to the end of the **present stem** of each **verb.**

Example: ۱ – تابیدن /tǎ.bi.dan/ (to shine)

(shining) تابان _____ = ان + تاب _____

۲ – خندیدن /kan.di.dan/ (to laugh)

(laughing) _____ = _____ + _____

۳– **نالیدن** /nǎ.li.dan/ (to moan)

(moaning) _____ = _____ + _____

۴– **لنگیدن** /lan.gi.dan/ (to limp)

(limping) _____ = _____ + _____

۵– **ترسیدن** /tar.si.dan/ (to fear)

(fearful) _____ = _____ + _____

۶– **لرزیدن** /lar.zi.dan/ (to shake)

(shaky) _____ = _____ + _____

3.4 Fill in the blank in each of the following sentences with the most appropriate **adjective** from the choices given in parentheses.

Example:

۱– خانه ی ما، <u>بزرگ ترین</u> خانه ی این کوچه است. (بزرگ ترین – سرد – نادان)

/kǎ.ne.ye- mǎ- ... - kǎ.ne.ye- in- ku.če- ast/ (/bo.zorg.ta.rin/- /sard/- /nǎ.dǎn/)

Our house is <u>the biggest</u> house in this alley. (the biggest – cold – ignorant)

٢- فرانسه، یک کشورِ ــــــــــ است. (بخشنده ترین – اُروپایی – قرمز)

/fa.răn.se- yek- keš.va.re- ... - ast/ (/baǩ.šan.de.ta.rin/-/o.ru.pă.yi/- /ǧer.mez/)

France is a _____ country. (most generous – European – red)

٣- دخترت بسیار ــــــــــ است. (زیبا – بلندترین – سفیدتر)

/doǩ.ta.rat- bes.yăr- ... - ast/ (/zi.bă/-/bo.land.ta.rin/-/se.fid.tar/)

Your daughter is very _____ . (beautiful – the tallest – whiter)

٤- رنگِ برف ــــــــــ است.(انگلیسی – شهری – سفید)

/ran.ge- barf- ... - ast/ (/en.ge.li.si/-/šah.ri/-/se.fid/)

The color of the snow is _____ . (English – urban – white)

٥- شاخه ی آن درخت ــــــــــ است. (شکسته – هفتگی – نابینا)

/šă.ǩe.ye- ăn- de.raǩt- ... - ast/ (/še.kas.te/-/haf.te.gi/-/nă.bi.nă/)

The branch of that tree is _____ . (broken – weekly – blind)

3.5 In the following sentences, change the nouns shown in the parentheses into the appropriate **adjectives** and rewrite the sentences.

Example: ١ – شوهرِ من (آمریکا) است.

/šo.ha.re- man- (ăm.ri.kă)- ast/

My husband is American.

شوهرِ من آمریکایی است.

۲- این کتاب به زبانِ (انگلیس) است.

/in-ke.tăb- be- za.bă.ne- (en.ge.lis)- ast/
This book is in English.

۳- من دوست دارم زبانِ (فارس) را یاد بگیرم.

/man- dust- dă.ram- za.bă.ne- (fărs)- ră- yăd- be.gi.ram/
I like to learn the Persian language.

۴- یادگیری زبانِ (ایتالیا) از زبانِ (آلمان) ساده تر است.

/yăd.gi.ri.ye- za.bă.ne- (i.tă.li.yă)- az- za.bă.ne- (ăl.măn)- să.de.tar- ast/
The Italian language is easier to learn than the German language.

۵- من دوستانِ (مکزیک) بسیاری دارم.

/man- dus.tă.ne- (mek.zik)- bes.yă.ri- dă.ram/
I have a lot of Mexican friends.

۶- ایران، یک کشورِ (آسیا) است.

/i.răn- yek- keš.va.re- (ă.si.yă)- ast/
Iran is an Asian country.

٧- من (کانادا) هستم.

/man- (kǎ.nǎ.dǎ)- has.tam/
I am Canadian.

3.6 Form **adjectives** using the **past stems of the verbs** by adding the suffix ه — ـه /e/.
Write the words on the lines to complete the **adjective** column in the table below.

Adjective	Past Stem	Infinitive
Example: شِکَسته (broken)	شِکست	شِکستن (to break) /še.kas.tan/
_____ (closed)	بَست	بَستن (to close) /bas.tan/
_____ (eaten)	خورد	خوردن (to eat) /ḱor.dan/

_____ (seen)	دید	**دیدن** (to see) /di.dan/
_____ (told)	گُفت	**گُفتن** (to tell) /gof.tan/
_____ (heard)	شنید	**شنیدن** (to hear) /še.ni.dan/
_____ (stayed)	ماند	**ماندن** (to stay) /măn.dan/

_____ (done)	کرد	کردن (to do) /kar.dan/
_____ (gone)	رفت	رفتن (to go) /raf.tan/
_____ (cooked)	پخت	پختن (to cook) /poǩ.tan/
_____ (polluted)	آلود	آلودن (to pollute) /ǎ.lu.dan/

3.7 Turn the following **adjectives** into the **comparative form** by adding the suffix تر

/tar/ to the end of the **adjectives**.

Example: بزرگ تر = تر + بزرگ
/bo.zorg/
(big)

_____ = _____ + کوچک
/ku.čak/
(small)

_____ = _____ + سفید
/se.fid/
(white)

_____ = _____ + سیاه
/si.yăh/
(black)

_____ = _____ + شکسته
/še.kas.te/
(broken)

_____ = _____ + شاد
/šăd/
(happy)

_____ = _____ +   آرام
/ă.răm/
(quiet)

_____ = _____ +   بلند
/bo.land/
(long/tall)

_____ = _____ +   نرم
/narm/
(soft)

_____ = _____ +   زیبا
/zi.bă/
(beautiful)

_____ = _____ +   تابان
/tă.băn/
(shining)

118

CHAPTER 4

ADVERBS

قيدها

‎ُ
/ğeyd.hă/

Adverbs describe verbs, adjectives or other adverbs. They are generally classifies as either *"simple adverbs"* or *"compound adverbs"* based on their structures.

- Simple Adverbs:
These adverbs take the form of one word.

EXAMPLES:

never /har.gez/ هرگز

well /ḱub/ خوب

soft /narm/ نرم

- Compound Adverbs:
These adverbs take the form of more than one element (a noun, an adjective, a preposition, a prefix or a suffix).

119

EXAMPLES:

recently   /be- tă.ze.gi/   به تازگی

everywhere   /ha.me- jă/   همه جا

luckily   /ǩoš.baǩ.tă.ne/   خوشبختانه

Adverbs may also be divided into the following nine groups based on their individual meaning or function in a sentence:

1) Adverbs of Time   2) Adverbs of Place
3) Adverbs of Quantity   4) Adverbs of Quality
5) Descriptive Adverbs   6) Adverbs of Repetition
7) Repetitive Adverbs   8) Adverbs of Gradation
9) Negative Adverbs

   1) Adverbs of Time

EXAMPLES:

this year   /em.săl/   امسال

Tuesday   /se- šan.be/   سه شنبه

sometimes   /gă.hi- o.ğăt/   گاهی اوقات

2) Adverbs of Place

EXAMPLES:

here   /in.jă/   اینجا

there   /ăn.jă/   آنجا

everywhere   /ha.me- jă/   همه جا

3) Adverbs of Quantity

EXAMPLES:

a lot   /ǩey.li/   خیلی

a bit   /ka.mi/   کمی

some   /meğ.dă.ri/   مقداری

4) Adverbs of Quality

EXAMPLES:

softly   /be- nar.mi/   به نرمی

fast   /tond/   تند

well   /ǩub/   خوب

5) Descriptive Adverbs:

This group of adverbs describes the state and condition of the *subject* or *object* in a sentence. The most common *descriptive adverbs* are:

❖ Descriptive adverbs that are formed by adding the suffix انه /ǎ.ne/ to the end of an adjective.

EXAMPLES:

luckily   /ǩoš.baǩ.tǎ.ne/   خوشبخت + انه = خوشبختانه

unfortunately   /mo.te.'as.se.fǎ.ne/   متأسّف + انه = متأسّفانه

victoriously   /pi.ruz.man.dǎ.ne/   پیروزمند + انه = پیروزمندانه

❖ Descriptive adverbs that are formed by adding the preposition با /bǎ/ or به /be/ to the beginning of a noun.

EXAMPLES:
- prefix با + noun :

beautifully   /bǎ.zi.bǎ.yi/   با + زیبایی = با زیبایی

with joy   /bǎ.ǩoš.hǎ.li/   با + خوشحالی = با خوشحالی

anxiously   /bǎ.ne.ga.rǎ.ni/   با + نگرانی = با نگرانی

- prefix به + noun :

slowly   /be.ǎ.rǎ.mi/   به + آرامی = به آرامی

easily   /be.rǎ.ha.ti/   به + راحتی = به راحتی

alone   /be.tan.hǎ.yi/   به + تنهایی = به تنهایی

121

❖   Adverbs that are basically "adjectives" but are used to describe verbs.

They could be *"simple"* (made out of one word) or *"compound"* (made out of more than one element).

EXAMPLES:

- for *"simple"*:

كامپیوتر من خوب کار می کند.

/kăm.pi.yu.te.re- man- ḵub- kăr- mi.ko.nad/

My computer works <u>well</u>.

من آرام روی زمین نشستم.

/man- ă.răm- ru.ye- za.min- ne.šas.tam/

I sat on the floor <u>slowly</u>.

مادرم خندان وارد شد.

/mă.da.ram- ḵan.dăn- vă.red- šod/

My mother came in <u>smiling</u>.

- for *"compound"* :

سارا با حوصله به من گوش داد.

/să.ră- bă.ho.se.le- be- man- guš- dăd/

Sara <u>patiently</u> listened to me.

آنها با دقّت نامه را خواندند.

/ăn.hă- bă.değ.ğat- nă.me- ră- ḵăn.dand/

They <u>carefully</u> read the letter.

مریم تندتر آمد.

/mar.yam- tond.tar- ă.mad/

Maryam came <u>faster</u>.

6) Adverbs of Repetition

EXAMPLES:

again   /băz/   باز

again   /do.bă.re/   دوباره

also   /ham/   هَم

once again   /bǎ.re- di.gar/   بارِ دیگر

7) Repetitive Adverbs

(These adverbs form by repeating an adverb.)

EXAMPLES:

very fast   /tond- tond/   تند تند

very slowly   /ǎ.rǎm- ǎ.rǎm/   آرام آرام

little by little   /kam- kam/   کم کم

8) Adverbs of Gradation

EXAMPLES:

day by day   /ruz- be- ruz/   روز به روز

minute by minute   /da.ǧi.ǧe- be- da.ǧi.ǧe/   دقیقه به دقیقه

house to house   /ǩǎ.ne- be- ǩǎ.ne/   خانه به خانه

9) Negative Adverbs

EXAMPLES:

never   /har.gez/   هرگز

not at all   /as.lan/   اصلاً

no way   /be.hič.vajh/   بهیچوجه

● Arabic Adverbs

These are the adverbs that have entered into the Persian language from Arabic and they all end in   اً   /an/ *(tanvin)*.

EXAMPLES:

right away   /fo.ran/   فوراً

probably   /eh.te.mǎ.lan/   احتمالاً

definitely   /hat.man/   حتماً

Chapter 4 – Vocabulary

آ

very slowly	آرام آرام
to cook	آشپزی کردن
knowingly	آگاهانه
to come	آمدن
there	آنجا

ا

room	اتاق
probably	احتمالاً
from	از
to wake up	از خواب بیدار شدن
not at all	اصلاً
today	امروز
this year	امسال
Iran	ایران
here	اینجا

ب

patiently	با حوصله
happily/with joy	با خوشحالی
carefully	با دقّت
rain	باران
once again	بار دیگر
to rain	باریدن

again	باز
to open	باز کردن
beautifully	با زیبایی
with joy/ with excitement	با شوق
kindly	با محبّت
anxiously	با نگرانی
child	بچّه
without a doubt	بدون تردید
brother	برادر
to return	برگشتن
to plan	برنامه ریختن
very	بسیار
slowly	به آرامی
recently	به تازگی
alone	به تنهایی
easily	به راحتی
shortly	به زودی
softly	به نرمی
no way	بهیچوجه
impatiently	بی صبرانه
to come out	بیرون آمدن

پ

father	پدر
mailman	پستچی
boy/son	پسر

victorious	پیروزمندانه

ت

Turkey	ترکیه
car crash	تصادف
decision	تصمیم
to make decisions/ to decide	تصمیم گرفتن
to call	تلفن زدن
all	تمام
fast	تند
very fast	تند تند
alone	تنها

ج

box	جعبه
to fight	جنگیدن

ح

certainly	حتماً
truly	حقیقتاً

خ

house/home	خانه
house to house	خانه به خانه
smiling	خندان
to read	خواندن
well/good	خوب
fortunately	خوشبختانه

very	خیلی

د

to give	دادن
girl/daughter	دختر
door/in	در
enemy	دشمن
minute by minute	دقیقه به دقیقه
to miss someone	دل کسی برای کسی تنگ شدن
again	دوباره
late	دیر
yesterday	دیروز
last night	دیشب

ر

to treat/to behave	رفتار کردن
to go	رفتن
day by day	روز به روز
on/on top of	رویِ

ز

to get injured	زخمی شدن
floor/ground	زمین
early	زود

س

year	سال

fast	سریع
trip	سفر
Tuesday	سه‌شنبه

ش

student	شاگرد
bravely	شجاعانه
to wash	شستن

ص

patiently	صبورانه

ظ

dish	ظرف

ف

to forget	فراموش کردن
tomorrow	فردا
right away	فوراً

ق

adverb	قید

ک

to work/to function	کار کردن
computer	کامپیوتر
key	کلید
to help	کمک کردن
little by little	کم کم

a bit/ a little	کمی

گ

sometimes	گاهی
sometimes	گاهی اوقات
to put/ to place	گذاشتن
crying/in tears	گریان
to tell/to say	گفتن
to listen	گوش دادن

م

mother	مادر
car	ماشین
unfortunately	متأسّفانه
respectfully	محترمانه
man	مرد
school	مدرسه
excitedly	مشتاقانه
problem/ difficult	مشکل
to apologize	معذرت خواستن
some	مقداری
to wait	منتظر بودن
party	مهمانی

ن

letter	نامه
soft	نرم
to sit	نشستن

۵

gift	هدیه
every day	هر روز
never	هرگز
consciously	هشیارانه
last week	هفته ی گذشته
also	هم
everywhere	همه جا
always	همیشه
artistically	هنرمندانه

Test Yourself:

4.1 Find the **adverbs** in the sentences below and write them in the spaces provided. The number of existing **adverbs** in each sentence has been indicated in the parentheses.

Example:

۱- من هرگز تو را فراموش نخواهم کرد. (۱)

/man- har.gez- to- ră- fa.ră.muš- na.ǩă.ham- kard/
I will never forget you.

هرگز

۲- دیشب از مهمانی دیر برگشتیم. (۲)

/di.šab- az- meh.mă.ni- dir- bar.gaš.tim/
We returned late from the party last night.

_____ _____

۳- خوشبختانه امروز باران نخواهد بارید. (۲)

/ǩoš.baǩ.tă.ne- em.ruz- bă.răn- na.ǩă.had- bă.rid/
Luckily, it will not rain today.

_____ _____

۴– دیروز سارا احتمالاً باخوشحالی به مدرسه رفت.(۳)

/di.ruz- sǎ.rǎ- eh.te.mǎ.lan- bǎ.ǩoš.hǎ.li- be- mad.re.se- raft/

Yesterday, Sara probably happily went to school.

_____ _____ _____

۵– من همیشه تنها کار می کنم.(۲)

/man- ha.mi.še- tan.hǎ- kǎr- mi.ko.nam/

I always work alone.

_____ _____

۶– فردا زود از خواب بیدار خواهم شد. (۲)

/far.dǎ- zud- az- ǩǎb- bi.dǎr- ǩǎ.ham- šod/

I will wake up early tomorrow.

_____ _____

۷– کامپیوترم سریع و خوب کار می کند.(۲)

/kǎm.pi.yu.te.ram- sa.ri ʻ – va- ǩub- kǎr- mi.ko.nad/

My computer works fast and well.

_____ _____

129

۸– سارا بدون تردید امروز می آید.(۲)

/să.ră- be.du.ne- tar.did- em.ruz- mi.ă.yad/

Sara without a doubt comes today.

_____ _____

4.2 Rewrite each sentence by changing the **adjective** in the parentheses into an **adverb.**

Example: ۱– شاگردانِ من (صبور) منتظرِ من بودند.

/šă.ger.dă.ne- man- (sa.bur)- mon.ta.ze.re- man- bu.dand/

My students were waiting for me (patient).

شاگردانِ من صبورانه منتظرِ من بودند.

۲– آنها (شجاع) با دشمن جنگیدند.

/ăn.hă- (šo.jă')- bă- doš.man- jan.gi.dand/

They fought with the enemy (brave).

_____

۳– ما (مشتاق) برای سفرمان به ترکیه برنامه ریختیم.

/mă- (moš.tăğ)- ba.ră.ye- sa.fa.re.măn- be- tor.ki.ye- bar.nă.me- riǩ.tim/

We planned for our trip to Turkey (excited).

_____

130

۴- سارا (خوشبخت) در تصادف زخمی نشده است.

/să.ră- (ǩoš.baǩt)- dar- ta.să.dof- zaǩ.mi- na.šo.de- ast/
(fortunate) Sara has not been injured in the crash.

۵- دخترمن (آگاه) این تصمیم را گرفته است.

/doǩ.ta.re- man- (ă.găh)- in- tas.mim- ră- ge.ref.te- ast/
My daughter has made this decision (knowing).

۶- سینا (هشیار) به من گوش داد.

/si.nă- (hoš.yăr)- be- man- guš- dăd/
Sina listened to me (conscious).

۷- تو (هنرمند) آشپزی می کنی.

/to- (ho.nar.mand)- ăš.pa.zi- mi.ko.ni/
You cook (artistic).

۸- با ما بسیار (محترم) رفتار کردند.

/bă- mă- bes.yăr- (moh.ta.ram)- raf.tăr- kar.dand/
[They] treated us very (respectful).

4.3 Choose the word that is an **adverb of time** from the choices provided in parentheses. Then, rewrite the sentences in the spaces provided.

Example:

١- پسرم ـــــــ مشکل را به من گفت. (دیروز- به آرامی- تند)

/pe.sa.ram- _____ - moš.kel- rǎ- be- man- goft/ (di.ruz-/-be.ǎ.rǎ.mi/-/tond/

My son told me [about] the issue _____.(yesterday- slowly- fast)

پسرم دیروز مشکل را به من گفت.

٢- بچّه ها ـــــــ از اتاق بیرون خواهند آمد.(خندان- به زودی- شاید)

/bač.če.hǎ- _____ - az- o.tǎǧ- bi.run- kǎ.hand- ǎ.mad/(/kan.dǎn/-/be.zu.di/-/šǎ.yad/)

The children will come out of the room _____. (smiling- shortly- maybe)

٣- من ـــــــ کلید را به آن مرد دادم.(بسیار- حتماً- دیشب)

/man- _____ ke.lid- rǎ- be- ǎn- mard- dǎ.dam/(/bes.yǎr/-/hat.man/-/di.šab/)

I gave the key to that man _____. (very- certainly- last night)

٤- سینا ـــــــ به من تلفن می زند. (با محبّت- گریان- گاهی)

/si.nǎ- _____ be- man- te.le.fon- mi.za.nad/(/bǎ.mo.hab.bat/-/ger.yǎn/- /gǎ.hi/)

Sina _____ calls me. (kindly- in tears- sometimes)

۵- پستچی _____ جعبه ها را روی زمین می گذارد.(هر روز- تند- کمی)

/post.či- _____ - jaʿ.be.hǎ- rǎ- ru.ye- za.min- mi.go.zǎ.rad/(/har-ruz/-/tond/-/ka.mi/)

The mailman places the boxes on the floor _____.(every day-fast-a little)

4.4 Fill in the blanks with the most appropriate **adverb** from the choices provided in the parentheses.

Example:

۱- ما ‌‌‌هفته ی گذشته از سفر برگشتیم. (هفته ی گذشته- با محبّت)

/mǎ- ... - az- sa.far- bar.gaš.tim/ (/haf.te.ye- go.zaš.te/-/bǎ.mo.hab.bat/)
We came back from the trip_____. (last week – kindly)

۲- سام _____ به من کمک می کند. (حتماً – دیشب)

/sǎm- ... - be- man- ko.mak- mi.ko.nad/ (/hat.man/-/di.šab/)
Sam _____ helps me. (definitely – last night)

۳- سارا _____ تمام ظرف ها را شست. (خیلی – به تنهایی)

/sǎ.rǎ- ... - ta.mǎ.me- zarf.hǎ- rǎ- šost/ (/ǩey.li/-/be.tan.hǎ.yi/)
Sara washed all the dishes _____ . (very – alone)

۴- _____ پدرم به ایران برگشت. (متأسّفانه – کمی)

/... - pe.da.ram- be- i.răn- bar.gašt/ (/mo.te.ʿas.se.fă.ne/-/ka.mi/)
_____ my father returned to Iran. (unfortunately – a little bit)

۵- سینا _____ هدیه اش را باز کرد. (با شوق – خیلی)

/si.nă- ... - had.ye.aš- ră- băz- kard/ (/bă.šoğ/-/ǩey.li/)
Sina opened his present _____ . (with joy – very)

۶- من از شما _____ معذرت می خواهم. (حقیقتاً – سال گذشته)

/man- az- šo.mă- ... - maʿ.ze.rat- mi.ǩă.ham/ (/ha.ği.ğa.tan/-/să.le- go.zaš.te/)
I _____ apologize to you. (truly– last year)

۷- پدر و مادرم _____ در را باز کردند. (فردا – به آرامی)

/pe.dar- va- mă.da.ram- ... - dar- ră- băz- kar.dand/ (/far.dă/-/be.ă.ră.mi/)
My father and mother _____ opened the door. (tomorrow – slowly)

۸- من _____ دلم برای سارا تنگ شده است. (فردا – کمی)

/man- ... - de.lam- ba.ră.ye- să.ră- tang- šo.de- ast/ (/far.dă/-/ka.mi/)
I've missed Sara _____ . (tomorrow – a little bit)

۹- برادرم _____ به خانه آمد. (دیر - خوب)

/ba.rǎ.da.ram- ... - be- ǩǎ.ne- ǎ.mad/ (/dir/- /ǩub/)
My brother came home _____ . (late – well)

۱۰- ماشین من _____ کار می کند. (بی صبرانه - خوب)

/mǎ.ši.ne- man- ... - kǎr- mi.ko.nad/ (/bi.sab.rǎ.ne/-/-/ǩub/)
My car works _____ . (impatiently – well)

CHAPTER 5

PREPOSITIONS

حروف اضافه

/ho.ru.fe- e.ză.fe/

Prepositions are the words that relate other words to the verb in a sentence. They usually appear before the nouns or pronouns in a sentence, or are part of the formation of the adjectives, adverbs, prefix verbs or phrasal verbs. They could be divided into two groups: *"simple prepositions"* and *"compound prepositions"*.

- Simple Prepositions:

These prepositions take the form of one word. The most common *simple prepositions* are:

(to) /be/ به

(in) /dar/ در

(from) /az/ از

(with) /bǎ/ با

(without) /bi/ بی

(until) /tǎ/ تا

(for) /ba.rǎ.ye/ برای

(without) /be.du.ne/ بدون

- Compound Prepositions:

These prepositions take the form of more than one word. Some *simple prepositions* join other words to form *compound prepositions*. The most common *compound prepositions* are:

(except for) /be- joz/ به جز

(except for) /be- ğeyr- az/ به غیر از

(at the moment of) /be- mah.ze/ به محض

(because of) /be- kǎ.te.re/ به خاطر

(during) /dar- mod.da.te/ در مدّت

(as a result of) /dar- na.ti.je.ye/ در نتیجه ی

(before) /ğabl- az/ قبل از

(after) /ba'd- az/ بعد از

Note:

Prepositions might have different meanings based on their role in a sentence; they may also change meanings when combined with other words.

EXAMPLES:

- the preposition به /be/:

ما به پاریس رفتیم.

/mǎ- be- pǎ.ris- raf.tim/

We went <u>to</u> Paris.

این کتاب به زبان فارسی است.

/in- ke.tăb- be- za.bă.ne- făr.si- ast/
This book is <u>in</u> Persian.

مریم جعبه را به راحتی باز کرد.

/mar.yam- ja '.be- ră- be- ră.ha.ti- băz- kard/
Maryam opened the box <u>easily</u>. (part of an adverb)

سام با ماشینش به درخت خورد.

/săm- bă- mă.ši.naš- be- de.rakt- kord/
Sam <u>bumped into</u> a tree with his car. (part of a phrasal verb)

پسرم بشقابش را به زمین انداخت.

/pe.sa.ram- boš.ğă.baš- ră- be- za.min- an.dăkt/
My son dropped his plate <u>on</u> the floor.

من به تو حقیقت را گفتم.

/man- be- to- ha.ği.ğat- ră- gof.tam/
I told <u>you</u> the truth. (an indicator of indirect object)

به خاطر تو، این شغل را به من دادند.

/be- kă.te.re- to- in- šoğl- ră- be- man- dă.dand/
They gave me this job <u>because of</u> you. (in combination with another word)

به سمت جادّه ی اصلی بپیچ !

/be- sam.te- jăd.de.ye- as.li- be.pič/
Turn <u>toward</u> the main road! (in combination with another word)

به محض ورود، پرچم را دیدم.

/be- mah.ze- vo.rud- par.čam- ră- di.dam/
<u>At the moment of</u> arrival, I saw the flag. (in combination with another word)

همه آمدند، به جز لیلا.

/ha.me- ă.ma.dand- be- joz- ley.lă/
Everybody came, <u>except for</u> Leila. (in combination with another word)

به وسیله ی پست اکسپرس کتاب را برایت خواهم فرستاد.

/be- va.si.le.ye- pos.te- eks.pe.res- ke.tăb- ră- ba.ră.yat- kă.ham- fe.res.tăd/
I will send you the book <u>by</u> express mail. (in combination with another word)

من از این سفر، هیچ چیزی به دست نیاوردم.

/man- az- in- sa.far- hič- či.zi- be- dast- na.yă.var.dam/

I did not <u>gain</u> anything from this trip. (part of a phrasal verb)

- the preposition در /dar/:

پدرم در ایران زندگی می کند.

/pe.da.ram- dar- i.răn- zen.de.gi- mi.ko.nad/

My father lives <u>in</u> Iran.

من در بالای آن کوه، کلبه ای دارم.

/man- dar- bă.lă.ye- ăn- kuh- kol.be.i- dă.ram/

I have a cabin <u>on</u> top of that mountain.

در زیر لایه های خاک، دانه ای داشت رشد می کرد.

/dar- zi.re- lă.ye.hă.ye- kăk- dă.ne.i- dăšt- rošd- mi.kard/

<u>Underneath</u> the layers of soil, a seed was growing.

ما در مدرسه با هم آشنا شدیم.

/mă- dar- mad.re.se- bă- ham- ă.še.nă- šo.dim/

We met each other <u>at</u> school.

شما به یک عکس دو اینچ در سه اینچ احتیاج دارید.

/šo.mă- be- yek- ak.se- do- inč- dar- se- inč- eh.ti.yăj- dă.rid/

You need a two inch <u>by</u> three inch photo.

مریم یک روز در میان به من تلفن می زند.

/mar.yam- yek- ruz- dar- mi.yăn- be- man- te.le.fon- mi.za.nad/

Maryam calls me <u>every other day</u>. (part of an adverb)

در نتیجه ی سرما، جادّه ها بسته هستند.

/dar- na.ti.je.ye- sar.mă- jăd.de.hă- bas.te- has.tand/

<u>As the result of</u> cold weather, the roads are closed.

- the preposition از /az/:

من دارم از خانه ی سارا می آیم.

/man- dă.ram- az- kă.ne.ye- să.ră- mi.ă.yam/

I am coming <u>from</u> Sara's house.

پسرت بلندتر از پسر من است.

/pe.sa.rat- az- pe.sa.re- man- bo.land.tar- ast/
Your son is taller <u>than</u> my son.

از سال ۱۹۹۰، این موزه بسته است.

/az- să.le- he.ză.ro- noh.sa.do- na.vad- in- mu.ze- bas.te- ast/
<u>Since</u> 1990, this museum has been closed.

تمام ثروتم را در قُمار از دست دادم.

/ta.mă.me- ser.va.tam- ră- dar- ğo.măr- az- dast- dă.dam/
[I] <u>lost</u> all my wealth in gambling. (part of a phrasal verb)

ما هیچوقت به خارج از کشور سفر نکرده ایم.

/mă- hič.vağt- be- kă.rej- az- keš.var- sa.far- na.kar.de.im/
We have never traveled <u>outside</u> of the country.

گردنبند من از طلاست.

/gar.dan.ban.de- man- az- ta.lăst/
My necklace is <u>made of</u> gold.

از روی کنجکاوی، در صندوقچه را باز کردیم.

/az- ru.ye- konj.kă.vi- da.re- san.duğ.če- ră- băz- kar.dim/
<u>Out of</u> curiosity, [we] opened the chest.

یکی از شما پنجره ی من را شکسته است.

/ye.ki- az- šo.mă- pan.je.re.ye- man- ră- še.kas.te- ast/
One <u>of</u> you has broken my window.

پدرم از هوای آلوده مریض شد.

/pe.da.ram- az- ha.vă.ye- ă.lu.de- ma.riz- šod/
My father got sick <u>because of</u> the polluted air.

از دیدن برادرت خوشحال شدم.

/az- di.da.ne- ba.ră.da.rat- koš.hăl- šo.dam/
[I] was happy <u>to</u> see your brother.

حقیقت را از مریم بپرس !

/ha.ği.ğat- ră- az- mar.yam- be.pors/
Ask <u>Maryam</u> the truth! (an indicator of indirect object)

140

- the preposition با /bǎ/:

بچّه ها دارند با هم بازی می کنند.

/bač.če.hǎ- dǎ.rand- bǎ- ham- bǎ.zi- mi.ko.nand/

The children are playing <u>with</u> each other.

ما با احترام به آنها سلام کردیم.

/mǎ- bǎ- eh.te.rǎm- be- ǎn.hǎ- sa.lǎm- kar.dim/

We saluted them <u>with respect</u>. (part of an adverb)

دخترت خیلی باهوش است.

/doǩ.ta.rat- ǩey.li- bǎ.huš- ast/

Your daughter is very <u>smart</u>. (part of an adjective)

- the preposition بی /bi/:

سام بی دلیل عَصبانی است.

/sǎm- bi.da.lil- 'a.sa.bǎ.ni- ast/

Sam is angry <u>without any reason</u>. (part of an adverb)

این کهکشان بی انتها چه زیباست.

/in- kah.ka.šǎ.ne- bi.en.te.hǎ- če- zi.bǎst/

This <u>endless</u> galaxy is so beautiful. (part of an adjective)

- the preposition تا /tǎ/:

از ساعت ۸ تا ۱۰ صبح نمی توانی اینجا پارک کنی.

/az- sǎ.'a.te- hašt- tǎ- da.he- sobh- ne.mi.ta.vǎ.ni- in.jǎ- pǎrk- ko.ni/

You can't park here from 8 <u>to</u> 10 o'clock in the morning.

تا طلوع آفتاب نخوابیدم.

/tǎ- to.lu.'e- ǎf.tǎb- na.ǩǎ.bi.dam/

I didn't sleep <u>until</u> dawn.

تا آخر هفته هوا گرم تر خواهد شد.

/tǎ- ǎ.ǩa.re- haf.te- ha.vǎ- garm.tar- ǩǎ.had- šod/

<u>By</u> the end of the week, it will get warmer.

Keep in Mind: تا /tă/ may function as a conjunction instead of a preposition if it connects two sentences.

EXAMPLE:

به تو تلفن زدم تا بتوانی با من حرف بزنی.

/be- to- te.le.fon- za.dam- tă- be.ta.vă.ni- bă- man- harf- be.za.ni/

[I] called you <u>so that</u> you can talk to me. (connects two sentences)

Note:

Sometimes, when the preposition به /be/ is part of a compound preposition, the letter ﻪ disappears from the end of the word به /be/, and the letter ﺑ connects to the beginning of the next word.

EXAMPLES:

(by) /be- va.si.le.ye/   بوسيله ی   ⟵   به + وسيله ی

(because of) /be- ăă.te.re/   بِخاطرِ   ⟵   به + خاطرِ

Chapter 5 – Vocabulary

آ

end of the week	آخرِ هفته
to meet	آشنا شدن
polluted	آلوده
to come	آمدن

ا

to need	احتیاج داشتن
from	از
to lose	از دست دادن
out of	از رویِ
main	اصلی
to drop	انداختن
inch	اینچ

ب

with	با
with respect	با احترام
to open	باز کردن
to play	بازی کردن
smart	باهوش
child	بچّه
without	بدونِ
brother	برادر
for	برایِ
closed	بسته

plate	بشقاب
after	بعد از
long/tall	بلند
to	به
except for	به جز
because of	به خاطرِ
to bump into	به چیزی خوردن
to gain	به دست آوردن
easily	به راحتی
toward	به سمتِ
except for	به غیر از
at the moment of	به محض
by	به وسیله ی
without	بی
endless	بی انتها
without any reason	بی دلیل

پ

to park	پارک کردن
father	پدر
flag	پرچم
to ask	پرسیدن
express mail	پستِ اکسپرس
son/boy	پسر
window	پنجره
to turn/to wrap	پیچیدن

	ت
until	تا
to call	تلفن زدن
all	تمام
to be able to/can	توانستن

	ث
wealth	ثروت

	ج
road	جادّه
box	جعبه

	ح
preposition	حرفِ اضافه
to talk	حرف زدن
truth	حقیقت

	خ
outside of	خارج از
soil	خاک
home/house	خانه
to sleep	خوابیدن
happy	خوشحال

	د
to give	دادن
to have	داشتن

seed	دانه
daughter/girl	دختر
in/door	در
on top of	در بالایِ
tree	درخت
underneath	در زیرِ
during	در مدّتِ
as the result of	در نتیجه ی
to see	دیدن
two	دو

	ر
to grow	رشد کردن
to go	رفتن

	ز
language/tongue	زبان
floor/ground	زمین
to live	زندگی کردن
beautiful	زیبا

	س
o'clock/clock/watch	ساعت
year	سال
trip	سفر
to salute/to say hello	سلام کردن
three	سه

	galaxy	کهکشان

ش

job	شغل
to break	شکستن

ص

morning	صبح
chest/small box	صندوقچه

ط

gold	طلا
dawn/sunrise	طلوعِ آفتاب

ع

angry	عصبانی
photo/picture	عکس

ف

Persian/Farsi	فارسی
to send	فرستادن

ق

before	قبل از
gambling	قمار

ک

book	کتاب
cabin	کلبه
curiosity	کنجکاوی
mountain	کوه

گ

necklace	گردنبند
warm	گرم
to tell/to say	گفتن

ل

layer	لایه

م

car	ماشین
school	مدرسه
sick	مریض
museum	موزه

و

arrival	ورود

ه

everyone/all	همه
air	هوا
nothing	هیچ چیز
never	هیچوقت

ی

every other day	یک روز در میان

Test Yourself:

5.1 Underline the **prepositions** in the sentences below and then write them on the lines provided. The number of existing **prepositions** in each sentence has been indicated in the parentheses.

Example:

۱ – من از مدرسه به خانه آمدم. (۲)

/man- az- mad.re.se- be- kǎ.ne- ǎ.ma.dam/
I came home from school.

از   به
_____   _____

۲ – سینا به جز من دوستی ندارد. (۱)

/si.nǎ- be.joz- man- dus.ti- na.dǎ.rad/
Sina does not have any friend except me.

_____

۳ – شما در ایران با چه کسی زندگی می کردید؟ (۲)

/šo.mǎ- dar- i.rǎn- bǎ- če- ka.si- zen.de.gi- mi.kar.did/
With whom were you living in Iran?

_____   _____

146

۴- از شمال تا جنوب پارک با سارا قدم زدم. (۳)

/az- šo.măl- tă- jo.nu.be- părk- bă- să.ră- ğa.dam- za.dam/

[I] walked with Sara from the north of the park to the south.

_____ _____ _____

۵- برای من چه خریده ای؟ (۱)

/ba.ră.ye- man- če- ǩa.ri.de.i/

What have you bought for me?

_____

۶- رایان در روزِ تولّدِ زنش دستبندی از نقره برایِ او خرید. (۳)

/ră.yăn- dar- ru.ze- ta.val.lo.de- za.naš- dast.ban.di- az- noğ.re- ba.ră.ye- u- ǩa.rid/

On her birthday, Ryan bought a silver bracelet for his wife.

_____ _____ _____

۷- از دیدن خواهرت در مهمانیِ سارا خوشحال شدم. (۲)

/az- di.da.ne- ǩă.ha.rat- dar- meh.mă.ni.ye- să.ră- ǩoš.hăl- šo.dam/

[I] was happy to see your sister at Sara's party.

_____ _____

147

CHAPTER 6

CONJUNCTIONS

حروف رَبط

/ho.ru.fe- rabt/

Conjuctions connect words or sentences. They are generally classified as *"simple conjunctions"* or *"compound conjunctions"*.

- Simple Conjunctions:
These conjunctions take the form of one word. The most common *simple conjunctions* are:

    (and) /va/ وَ

    (if) /a.gar/ اگر

    (but) /am.mă/ امّا

    (but) /va.li/ ولی

    (because) /zi.ră/ زیرا

    (because) /čon/ چون

(or) /yǎ/ یا

(that) /ke/ که

EXAMPLES:

من و سینا به پارک رفتیم.

/man- va- si.nǎ- be- pǎrk- raf.tim/

Sina <u>and</u> I went to the park.

اگر نیایی، ناراحت می شویم.

/a.gar- na.yǎ.yi- nǎ.rǎ.hat- mi.ša.vim/

[We] will be upset <u>if</u> [you] don't come.

مریم من را دید، امّا نشناخت.

/mar.yam- man- rǎ- did- am.mǎ- na.še.nǎkt/

Maryam saw me, <u>but</u> [she] did not recognize [me].

می خواهم بروم بخوابم، چون خیلی خسته هستم.

/mi.ǩǎ.ham- be.ra.vam- be.ǩǎ.bam- čon- ǩey.li- ǩas.te- has.tam/

[I] want to go to bed <u>because</u> [I] am very tired.

دوستت تلفن زد، نمی دانم سارا بود یا لیلا.

/dus.tat- te.le.fon- zad- ne.mi.dǎ.nam- sǎ.rǎ- bud- yǎ- ley.lǎ/

Your friend called; I don't know if it was Sara <u>or</u> Leila.

این ماشینی است که من تصمیم گرفته ام بخرم .

/in- mǎ.ši.ni- ast- ke- man- tas.mim- ge.ref.te.am- be.ǩa.ram/

This is the car <u>that</u> I have decided to buy.

- Compound Conjunctions:
These conjunctions take the form of more than one word. The most common *compound conjunctions* are:

(therefore) /dar- na.ti.je/ در نتیجه

(as soon as) /be- mah.zi- ke/ به محضی که

(even though) /a.gar- če/ اگر چه

(therefore) /ba.nǎ.bar.in/ بنابراین

(since) /az- vaǧ.ti- ke/ از وقتی که

(when) /vaǧ.ti/ وقتی

(even though) /bă.vo.ju.de- in.ke/ با وجود اینکه (با وجود این که)

(before) /ǧabl- az- in.ke/ قبل از اینکه (قبل از این که)

(after) /ba' d- az- in.ke/ بعد از اینکه (بعد از این که)

EXAMPLES:

فراموش کردم چراغ را خاموش کنم، در نتیجه لامپ سوخت.

/fa.ră.muš- kar.dam- če.răǧ- ră- ǩă.muš- ko.nam- dar- na.ti.je- lămp- suǩt/

[I] forgot to turn the light off; <u>therefore</u>, the bulb burned out.

به محضی که خبر را شنیدم، به تو تلفن زدم.

/be- mah.zi- ke- ǩa.bar- ră- še.ni.dam- be- to- te.le.fon- za.dam/

[I] called you <u>as soon as</u> [I] heard the news.

آپارتمانم خیلی کوچک بود، بنابراین فروختمش.

/ă.păr.te.mă.nam- ku.čak- bud- ba.nă.bar.in- fo.ruǩ.ta.maš/

My apartment was too small; <u>therefore</u>, [I] sold it.

از وقتی که طلاق گرفته ام، تنها زندگی می کنم.

/az- vaǧ.ti- ke- ta.lăǧ- ge.ref.te.am- tan.hă- zen.de.gi- mi.ko.nam/

[I] have lived alone <u>since</u> [I] got divorced.

وقتی رایان دانشجو بود، ما با هم دوست بودیم.

/vaǧ.ti- ră.yăn- dă.neš.ju- bud- mă- bă- ham- dust- bu.dim/

<u>When</u> Ryan was a student, we were friends.

بعد از اینکه تو را رساندم، به کتابخانه رفتم.

/ba'd- az- in.ke- to- ră- be- ǩă.ne- re.săn.dam- be- ke.tăb.ǩă.ne- raf.tam/

<u>After</u> [I] gave you a ride, [I] went to the library.

قبل از اینکه ظرف ها را بشویی، میز را تمیز کن!

/ǧabl- az- in.ke- zarf.hă- ră- be.šu.yi- miz- ră- ta.miz- kon/

Clean the table <u>before</u> washing the dishes!

Chapter 6 – Vocabulary

آ

apartment	آپارتمان
to come	آمدن

ا

room	اتاق
since	از وقتی که
if	اگر
even though	اگرچه
but	امّا
this year	امسال

ب

market	بازار
even though	با وجود اینکه
brother	برادر
snow	برف
to snow	برف آمدن
closed	بسته
after	بعد از اینکه
therefore	بنابراین
as soon as	به محضی که

پ

park	پارک

ت

to decide/ to make decisions	تصمیم گرفتن
closed	تعطیل
to call	تلفن زدن
to clean	تمیز کردن
alone/lonely	تنها
to be able to/can	توانستن

ج

to vacuum	جارو کردن

چ

light	چراغ
because	چون

خ

home/house	خانه
to turn off	خاموش کردن
news	خبر
to buy	خریدن
tired	خسته
to sleep	خوابیدن
to want	خواستن
very	خیلی

د

to know	دانستن

CONJUNCTIONS

college student	دانشجو
to knock on the door	در زدن
therefore	در نتیجه
to invite	دعوت کردن
friend	دوست
to see	دیدن
yesterday	دیروز

ر

to go	رفتن
to dance	رقصیدن

ز

to live	زندگی کردن
because	زیرا

س

to travel	سفر کردن
to burn	سوختن

ش

happy	شاد
to wash	شستن
to recognize	شناختن
to hear	شنیدن

ط

to get divorced	طلاق گرفتن

ظ

dish	ظرف

ف

to forget	فراموش کردن

ق

before	قبل از اینکه

ک

library	کتابخانه
To drive someone	کسی را رساندن
small	کوچک
that	که

ل

bulb	لامپ

م

car	ماشین
school	مدرسه
table/desk	میز

ن

upset	ناراحت

و

and	و
to enter/to come in	وارد شدن

when	وقتی
but	ولی

ه

excited	هیجان‌زده

ی

or	یا

Test Yourself:

6.1 Underline the **conjunctions** in the sentences below and write them in the spaces provided. The number of existing **conjunctions** in each sentence has been indicated in the parentheses.

Example:

۱– رایان و سارا امسال نتوانستند سفر کنند. (۱)

/ră.yăn- va- să.ră- em.săl- na.ta.vă.nes.tand- sa.far- ko.nand/
Ryan and Sara couldn't travel this year.

و

۲– به محضی که خانه را دیدم، هیجانزده و شاد شدم. (۲)

/be- mah.zi- ke- ǩa.ne- ră- di.dam- man- ham- ha.ye.jăn.za.de- va- šăd- šo.dam/
As soon as [I] saw the house, [I] became excited and happy.

_____   _____

۳– تو و دوستَت به بازار رفتید، امّا بازار بسته بود. (۲)

/to- va- dus.tat- be- bă.zăr- raf.tid- am.mă- bă.zăr- bas.te- bud/
You and your friend went to the market but the market was closed.

_____   _____

۴– سارا و پدرش در زدند، امّا من نشنیدم چون خواب بودم. (۳)

/să.ră- va- pe.da.raš- dar- za.dand- am.mă- man- na.še.ni.dam- čon- ǩăb- bu.dam/
Sara and her father knocked on the door, but I didn't hear them, because I was asleep.

_____   _____   _____

۵- در حالی که داشتم می رقصیدم، اتاق را جارو کردم. (۱)

/dar- hă.li- ke- dăš.tam- mi.rağ.si.dam- o.tăğ- ră- jă.ru- kar.dam/
While [I] was dancing, [I] vacuumed the room.

۶- دیروز برف آمد و در نتیجه مدرسه ها تعطیل بود. (۲)

/di.ruz- barf- ă.mad- va- dar- na.ti.je- mad.re.se.hă- ta'.til- bud/
It snowed yesterday and as a result schools were closed.

۷- من تو و لیلا را دعوت کردم، ولی شما نیامدید. (۲)

/man- to- va- ley.lă- ră- da'.vat- kar.dam- va.li- šo.mă- na.yă.ma.did/
I invited you and Leila, but you didn't come.

۸- وقتی تو و برادرت وارد شدید، من شما را نشناختم. (۲)

/vağ.ti- to- va- ba.ră.da.rat- vă.red- šo.did- man- šo.mă- ră- na.še.năḱ.tam/
When you and your brother walked in, I didn't recognize you.

CHAPTER 7

KASRE-YE EZĂFE:

THE VOWEL (◌ِ) /e/

The vowel ◌ِ /e/ *(kasre-ye ezăfe)* is used to connect various types of words.

    1) It connects a *noun* and the *adjective* describing it:

EXAMPLES:

اين كيفِ آبى را سام به من داده است.

/in- ki.fe- ă.bi- ră- săm- be- man- dă.de- ast/
Sam gave me this <u>blue bag</u>.

دخترانِ ايرانى زيبا هستند.

/doǩ.ta.ră.ne- i.ră.ni- zi.bă- has.tand/
<u>Iranian girls</u> are beautiful.

    2) It connects a *noun* and *detached possessive pronoun* related to it:

EXAMPLES:

دست من شکسته است.

/das.te- man- še.kas.te- ast/
My hand is broken.

مادران ما دارند می رقصند.

/mă.da.ră.ne- mă- dă.rand- mi.rağ.sand/
Our mothers are dancing.

3) It connects a *noun* and the *plural form of attached possessive pronoun* related to it:

EXAMPLES:

پسر تان دارد می دود.

/pe.sa.re.tăn- dă.rad- mi.da.vad/
Your*(pl)* son is running.

دوستانشان به مهمانی نیامدند.

/dus.tă.ne.šăn- be- meh.mă.ni- na.yă.ma.dand/
Their friends did not come to the party.

4) It connects two *nouns* to show a *possessive* relationship:

EXAMPLES:

ماشین های سارا قدیمی هستند.

/mă.šin.hă.ye- să.ră- ğa.di.mi- has.tand/
Sara's cars are old.

رنگ آنار سُرخ است.

/ran.ge- a.năr- sork- ast/
The pomegranate's color is red.

5) It connects two *adjectives*:

EXAMPLES:

در یک روز سرد برفی از خانه خارج شدیم.

/dar- yek- ru.ze- sar.de- bar.fi- az- kă.ne- kă.rej- šo.dim/
On a cold snowy day, we left the house.

157

ماه بزرگ نقره ای در آسمان می درخشد.

/mă.he- bo.zor.ge- noğ.re.i- dar- ă.se.man- mi.de.rak̆.šad/

The <u>big silver</u> moon is shining in the sky.

6) It connects a *preposition* to a *noun* or a *pronoun*:

EXAMPLES:

به خاطر سارا خانه را فروختم.

/be- k̆ă.te.re- să.ră- k̆ă.ne- ră- fo.ruk̆.tam/

[I] sold the house <u>because of Sara</u>.

به خاطر او خانه را فروختم.

/be- k̆ă.te.re- u- k̆ă.ne- ră- fo.ruk̆.tam/

[I] sold the house <u>because of her/him</u>.

Note:

If the word that carries the vowel ___ /e/ *(kasre-ye ezăfe)* ends in one of the following

three letters, the vowel ___ changes into ی /ye/:

- ا /ă/

- و /u/

- ه — ه /e/

EXAMPLES:

کتاب های تو سنگین هستند.

/ke.tăb.hă.ye- to- san.gin- has.tand/

<u>Your books</u> are heavy.

خانه ی ما در این جادّه است.

/k̆ă.ne.ye- mă- dar- in- jăd.de- ast/

<u>Our house</u> is on this road.

آرزوی من برآورده شد.

/ă.re.zu.ye- man- bar.ă.var.de- šod/

<u>My wish</u> came true.

158

Note:

In some Persian texts, word that ends in the letter ‍‍‍ه‍ ‍ — ه /e/ and carries a

vowel ___ /e/ *(kasre-ye ezăfe)* may not have the vowel ___ /e/ *(kasre-ye ezăfe)*

that changes into ی /ye/. Instead, you will see the Arabic symbol ء *(hamze),*

which sits on top of the letter ‍ه‍ — ه /e/ ; this turns it into ‍ۀ‍ — ۀ /ye/.

This is an orthographical case, and mostly seen in at least two-decade-old Persian texts.

Examples:

- older texts:

به خانۀ من خوش آمدید.

/be- kă.ne.ye- man- koš- ă.ma.did/
Welcome to <u>my house</u>.

- newer texts:

به خانه ی من خوش آمدید.

/be- kă.ne.ye- man- koš- ă.ma.did/
Welcome to <u>my house</u>.

159

Chapter 7 – Vocabulary

آ

blue	آبی
wish	آرزو
sky	آسمان
to come	آمدن

ا

| pomegranate | انار |

ب

open	باز
bad	بد
snowy	برفی
to come true	برآورده شدن
big	بزرگ
long/tall	بلند
to welcome some where	به جایی خوش آمدن
because of	به خاطرِ

پ

father	پدر
boy/son	پسر
window	پنجره
old	پیر

ج

| road | جادّه |

خ

to leave	خارج شدن
house/home	خانه
broken/out of order/spoiled	خراب

د

to give	دادن
daughter/girl	دختر
to shine	درخشیدن
to hurt	درد کردن
hand	دست
tooth	دندان
far	دور
friend	دوست
to run	دویدن
yesterday	دیروز

ر

to dance	رقصیدن
color	رنگ
day	روز

ز

| beautiful | زیبا |

	س
red	سرخ
cold	سرد
heavy	سنگین

	ش
to start	شروع شدن
to break	شکستن
broken	شکسته

	ط
gold	طلا

	ف
tomorrow	فردا
to sell	فروختن

	ق
old/ancient	قدیمی

	ک
book	کتاب
class/classroom	کلاس
bag	کیف

	گ
necklace	گردنبند

	م
mother	مادر
grandmother	مادر بزرگ
car	ماشین
month/moon	ماه
pencil	مداد
hair	مو
party	مهمانی

	ن
silver	نقره ای

Test Yourself:

7.1 Place the vowel ___ /e/ *(kasre-ye ezăfe)* between the **noun** and the **possessive pronoun** related to it in the following sentences and then rewrite the sentences. Pay attention to the words ending in letters that cause the vowel ___ /e/ *(kasre-ye ezăfe)* to change into ی /ye/.

Example:

۱- مادربزرگ من پیر است.

/mă.dar.bo.zorg- man- pir- ast/

My grandmother is old.

مادر بزرگ ِ من پیر است.

....

۲- کلاس ما فردا شروع می شود.

/ke.lăs- mă- far.dă- šo.ru' – mi.ša.vad/

Our class starts tomorrow.

....

۳- ماشین شما خراب است.

/mă.šin- šo.mă- ǩa.răb- ast/

Your car is broken.

....

۴- گردنبند تو از طلاست.

/gar.dan.band- to- az- ta.lăst/

Your necklace is made of gold.

. . . .

۵- من دیروز کتاب تو را پس دادم.

/man- di.ruz- ke.tăb- to- ră- pas- dă.dam/

I returned your book yesterday.

. . . .

۶- مداد او شکست.

/me.dăd- u- še.kast/

His/her pencil broke.

. . . .

۷- خانه آنها دور است.

/kă.ne- ăn.hă- dur- ast/

Their house is far away.

. . . .

۸- پنجره ها من باز هستند.

/pan.je.re.hă- man- băz- has.tand/

My windows are open.

....

۹- مو شما بلند است.

/mu- šo.mă- bo.land- ast/

Your hair is long.

....

۱۰- دندان او درد می کند.

/dan.dăn- u- dard- mi.ko.nad/

His/her tooth hurts.

....

۱۱- کیف ما سنگین است.

/kif- mă- san.gin- ast/

Our bag is heavy.

....

CHAPTER 8

DIRECT OBJECT INDICATOR : را /ră/

The "direct object indicator" را /ră/ comes after a *definite noun* or *detached pronoun* to show

that it has an "objective role" in a sentence. Only *direct objects* are followed by را /ră/.

EXAMPLES:

- When را /ră/ follows a *noun*:

اُستاد رایان را تشویق کرد.

/os.tăd- ră.yăn- ră- taš.viğ- kard/
The professor praised <u>Ryan</u>.

EXAMPLE:

- When را /ră/ follows a *pronoun* (detached):

دلقک ها ما را خنداندَند.

/dal.ğak.hă- mă- ră- ǩan.dăn.dand/
The clowns made <u>us</u> laugh.

165

EXAMPLE:

- When را /rǎ/ follows a *noun* and the *adjective* describing it:

سارا هوای سرد را دوست دارد.

/sǎ.rǎ- ha.vǎ.ye- sard- rǎ- dust- dǎ.rad/
Sara likes the <u>cold weather</u>.

EXAMPLE:

- When را /rǎ/ follows a *noun* and the multiple *adjectives* describing it:

سارا هوای سرد زمستانی را دوست دارد.

/sǎ.rǎ- ha.vǎ.ye- sar.de- ze.mes.tǎ.ni- rǎ- dust- dǎ.rad/
Sara likes the <u>cold wintry weather</u>.

EXAMPLE:

- When را /rǎ/ follows a *noun* and *detached possessive pronoun* related to it:

اُستاد نُمره ی من را تغییر داد.

/os.tǎd- nom.re.ye- man- rǎ- tağ.yir- dǎd/
The professor changed <u>my grade</u>.

EXAMPLE:

- When را /rǎ/ follows a *noun* and *attached possessive pronoun* related to it:

اُستاد نُمره ام را تغییر داد.

/os.tǎd- nom.re.am- rǎ- tağ.yir- dǎd/
The professor changed <u>my grade</u>.

EXAMPLE:

- When را /rǎ/ follows a *noun*, the *adjective* describing it and *detached possessive pronoun* related to it:

اُستاد نُمره ی بد من را تغییر داد.

/os.tǎd- nom.re.ye- ba.de- man- rǎ- tağ.yir- dǎd/
The professor changed <u>my bad grade</u>.

EXAMPLE:

- When را /rǎ/ follows a *noun*, the *adjective* describing it and *attached possessive pronoun* related to it:

اُستاد نُمره ی بَدَم را تغییر داد.

/os.tăd- nom.re.ye- ba.dam- ră- tağ.yir- dăd/
The professor changed <u>my bad grade</u>.

EXAMPLE:

- When را /ră/ follows a *noun* and the *possessive noun* related to it:

سگ سارا را دیده ام.

/sa.ge- să.ră- ră- di.de.am/
[I] have seen <u>Sara's dog</u>.

EXAMPLE:

- When را /ră/ follows a *noun*, the *adjective* describing it and the *possessive noun* related to it:

سگ سیاه سارا را دیده ام.

/sa.ge- si.yă.he- să.ră- ră- di.de.am/
[I] have seen <u>Sara's black dog</u>.

Note:

When you have more than one noun that function as *direct objects* in a sentence, you do not need to repeat را /ră/ after each of them. The را /ră/ comes after the final noun.

EXAMPLES:

من سارا و لیلا را می بینم.

/man- să.ră- va- ley.lă- ră- mi.bi.nam/
I see <u>Sara and Leila</u>.

من مادرها، پدرها و بچّه ها را می بینم.

/man- mă.dar.hă- pe.dar.hă- va- bač.če.hă- ră- mi.bi.nam/
I see <u>the mothers, the fathers and the children</u>.

Note:

The *"direct object indicator"* را /ră/ only follow *"detached pronouns as direct objects"*. If there are *"attached pronouns as direct objects"* in the sentence, they get attached to the end of the conjugated verb; and the *"direct object indicator"* را /ră/ is dropped from the sentence.

EXAMPLES:

- for *"detached pronoun as direct object"*:

تو را دیدم.

/to- rǎ- di.dam/

[I] saw <u>you</u>.

- for *"attached pronoun as direct object"*:

دیدمَت.

/di.da.mat/

[I] saw <u>you</u>.

Note:

The *"direct object indicator"* را /rǎ/ only follows *"definite nouns"*.

EXAMPLE:

پسرم سیب را خورد.

/pe.sa.ram- sib- rǎ- ǩord/

My son ate <u>the apple</u>.

- There are some **"exceptions"** to the above rule:

a) If a *definite noun* in the sentence refers to the item in general as opposed to a specific individual item, we should **avoid** using the *direct object indicator* را /rǎ/ after the noun.

EXAMPLES:

دخترم گیلاس دوست ندارد.

/doǩ.ta.ram- gi.lǎs- dust- na.dǎ.rad/

My daughter does not like <u>cherries</u>.

برای تولّدت دوچرخه می خواهی یا دوربین؟

/ba.rǎ.ye- ta.val.lo.dat- do.čar.ǩe- mi.ǩǎ.hi- yǎ- dur.bin/

Do you want <u>a bicycle</u> or <u>a camera</u> for your birthday?

b) If we have an *indefinite noun* as the object of the sentence and we are going to provide more information about it, we may **use** or **not use** the *direct object indicator* را /rǎ/ after the noun.

EXAMPLES:

- if we have a *definite noun* as the object of the sentence, then we use the *direct object indicator* را /rǎ/ after the noun:

من سگِ سیاه را دیدم.

/man- sa.ge- si.yăh- ră- di.dam/

I saw <u>the black dog</u>.

- if we have an *indefinite noun* as the object of the sentence, then we don't use the

direct object indicator را /ră/ after the noun:

من سگِ سیاهی دیدم.

/man- sa.ge- si.yă.hi- di.dam/

I saw <u>a black dog</u>.

- if we have an *indefinite noun* as the object of the sentence, but we are going to provide

more information about it, we may use or not use the *direct object indicator* را /ră/ after

the noun:

من سگِ سیاهی را دیدم که می لنگید.

/man- sa.ge- si.yă.hi- ră- di.dam- ke- mi.lan.gid/

I saw <u>a black dog</u> that was limping.

من سگِ سیاهی دیدم که می لنگید.

/man- sa.ge- si.yă.hi- di.dam- ke- mi.lan.gid/

I saw <u>a black dog</u> that was limping.

Chapter 8 – Vocabulary

آ

American	آمریکایی
to bring	آوردن

ا

professor	استاد
today	امروز

ب

must/have to	باید
for	برایِ
child	بچّه
bad	بد

پ

father	پدر
to give back/ to return	پس دادن
boy/son	پسر
to find	پیدا کردن
dress	پیراهن

ت

new/fresh	تازه
to type	تایپ کردن
to praise	تشویق کردن
to change	تغییر دادن
to close down	تعطیل کردن

all of	تمامِ
birthday	تولّد

خ

house/home	خانه
to make someone laugh	خنداندن
to want	خواستن
to eat	خوردن

د

to give	دادن
daughter/girl	دختر
to hurt	درد کردن
to invite	دعوت کردن
clown	دلقک
bicycle	دوچرخه
camera	دوربین
friend	دوست
to like/to love	دوست داشتن
to see	دیدن

ز

language/tongue	زبان
wintry	زمستانی

س

cold	سرد
dog	سگ

black	سیاه
apple	سیب

ش

to wash	شستن

ظ

dish	ظرف

ف

Persian/Farsi	فارسی
to forget	فراموش کردن

ق

to lend	قرض دادن

ک

computer	کامپیوتر

گ

necklace	گردنبند
cherry	گیلاس

ل

to limp	لنگیدن

م

mother	مادر
school	مدرسه
essay/article	مقاله

ن

grade/number	نمره

ه

yet	هنوز
air	هوا

Test Yourself:

8.1   In the sentences below, the **direct object indicator** را /rǎ/ has been eliminated on purpose. Find and underline the **object** of each sentence and then rewrite the sentence correctly by placing the **direct object indicator** را /rǎ/ in its appropriate place.

Example: ۱– پدر و مادرم تو به مهمانی شان دعوت کرده اند.

/pe.dar- va- mǎ.da.ram- to- be- meh.mǎ.ni.ye.šǎn- da'.vat- kar.de.and/
My father and mother have invited you to their party.

پدر و مادرم تو را به مهمانی شان دعوت کرده اند.

۲– باید تمامِ ظرف ها بشویم.

/bǎ.yad- ta.mǎ.me- zarf.hǎ- be.šu.yam/
[I] have to wash all the dishes.

۳– دوست داری پیراهنِ تازه ی من ببینی؟

/dust- dǎ.ri- pi.rǎ.ha.ne- tǎ.ze.ye- man- be.bi.ni/
Would [you] like to see my new dress?

۴- دوستِ آمریکاییِ من، زبان فارسی دوست دارد.

/dus.te- ăm.ri.kă.yi.ye- man- za.bă.ne- făr.si- dust- dă.rad/

My American friend likes the Persian language.

۵- امروز مدرسه ها تعطیل کرده اند.

/em.ruz- mad.re.se.hă- ta'.til- kar.de.and/

[They] have closed the schools today.

۶- کتابت به من قرض می دهی؟

/ke.tă.bat- be- man- ğarz- mi.da.hi/

Will [you] lend me your book?

۷- فراموش کردم کامپیوترم بیاورم.

/fa.ră.muš- kar.dam- kăm.pi.yu.te.ram- bi.yă.va.ram/

[I] forgot to bring my computer.

۸- هنوز مقاله ام تایپ نکرده ام.

/ha.nuz- ma.ğă.le.am- tăyp- na.kar.de.am/

[I] haven't typed my essay yet.

۹- ما مریم دیدیم.

/mă- mar.yam- di.dim/

We saw Maryam.

۱۰- دوستانم دوربینِ من پیدا نکردند.

/dus.tă.nam- dur.bi.ne- man- pey.dă- na.kar.dand/

My friends didn't find my camera.

۱۱- گردنبندت پس دادم.

/gar.dan.ban.dat- pas- dă.dam/

[I] returned your necklace.

CHAPTER 9

ARABIC SIGNS

نشانه های عربی

/ne.šă.ne.hă.ye- a.ra.bi/

These are the signs entered into the Persian language from the Arabic language.

- ّ *(tašdid)* is the "Gemination Mark". It sits on top of a letter to show that the letter should be pronounced twice.

EXAMPLES:

برادرم نقّاشِ مشهوری است.

/ba.ră.da.ram- naǧ.ǧă.še- maš.hu.ri- ast/

My brother is a famous <u>painter</u>.

رایان سکّه ها را آرام آرام شمُرد.

/rǎ.yǎn- sek.ke.hǎ- rǎ- ǎ.rǎm- ǎ.rǎm- še.mord/
Ryan counted the <u>coins</u> slowly.

ما متشکّریم !

/mǎ- mo.te.šak.ke.rim/
We are <u>thankful</u>!

- ٌ /an/ *(tanvin)* is an Arabic symbol that sits on top of the letter ا /ǎ/ and appears at the end of Arabic adverbs.

EXAMPLES:

فوراً به مادرت تلفن بزن !

/fo.ran- be- mǎ.da.rat- te.le.fon- be.zan/
Call your mother <u>right away</u>!

لطفاً قبل از شام، دست هایتان را بشویید.

/lot.fan- ğabl- az- šǎm- dast.hǎ.ye.tǎn- rǎ- be.šu.yid/
<u>Please</u> wash your hands before dinner.

واقعاً متأسّفم !

/va.ğe.an- mo.te.ʾas.se.fam/
I am <u>truly</u> sorry!

- ء /ʾ/ *(hamze)* is a glottal stop (similar to the sound of the letter ع – عـ):

It may sit on top of the following three letters in Arabic words, turning them into a glottal stop /ʾ/ :

- ا /ǎ/ turning it to أ

- و /u/ turning it to ؤ

- ـیـ /i/ turning it to ئـ

EXAMPLES:

من با سارا هیچ مَسأله ای ندارم.

/man- bǎ- sǎ.rǎ- hič- mas.ʾa.le.i- na.dǎ.ram/
I have no <u>problem</u> with Sara.

176

ما تمام پرسش ها را، مُؤَدّبانه جواب دادیم.

/mă- ta.mă.me- por.seš.hă- ră- mo.ʼad.da.bă.ne- ja.văb- dă.dim/
We answered all the questions <u>politely</u>.

من پائیز را دوست دارم.

/man- pă.ʼiz- ră- dust- dă.ram/
I like the <u>fall</u>.

Note:

When the ئ / ʼ / is followed by the letter ـی /i/ , it can be replaced by another

letter ـی /i/. As a result, the glottal stop disappears and the two consecutive

letters ییـ will now have the sound /yi/.

Examples:

من پاییز را دوست دارم.

/man- pă.yiz- ră- dust- dă.ram/
I like the <u>fall</u>.

Note:

The ء / ʼ / (hamze) also appears at the end of some Arabic words and is also
pronounced as a glottal stop.

Examples:

فعل، مُهم ترین جُزء در یک جمله است.

/feʼl- mo.hem.ta.rin- jozʼ – dar- yek- jom.le- ast/
The verb is the most important <u>element</u> in a sentence.

این شئ ، برای دانشمندان ناشناخته است.

/in- šeyʼ - ba.ră.ye- dă.neš.man.dăn- nă.še.năk.te- ast/
This <u>object</u> is unknown to scientists.

این مجسّمه، یکی از اشیاء باستانی در این موزه است.

/in- mo.jas.sa.me- ye.ki- az- aš.yăʼ e- băs.tă.ni- dar- in- mu.ze- ast/
This statue is one of the ancient <u>objects</u> in this museum.

Note:

In at least two-decade-old Persian texts, the ء / ' / *(hamze)* might be used to replace the

vowel ‿ /e/ *(kasre-ye ezăfe)* when the word carrying the vowel ‿ /e/ *(kasre-ye ezăfe)*

ends in the letter ه — ە /e/. In this case, the ء / ' / *(hamze)* does not act as a glottal stop

and it sounds like /ye/.

EXAMPLES:

به خانهٔ ما خوش آمدید.

/be- kă.ne.ye- mă- koš- ă.ma.did/
Welcome to <u>our house</u>.

Chapter 9 – Vocabulary

question	پرسش
regretful	پشیمان

ت

hill	تپّه
imagination	تخیّل
to thank	تشکّر کردن
thinking	تفکّر
piece	تکّه
to call	تلفن زدن
all of	تمامِ
entirely	تماماً
civilization	تمدّن
very fast	تند تند
attention	توجّه

آ

slow/slowly	آرام
very slowly	آرام آرام
celestial	آسمانی

ا

probably	احتمالاً
basically	اساساً
objects	اشیاء
tonight	امشب

ج

element/part	جزء
to answer	جواب دادن

ب

with respect/respectfully	با احترام
ancient	باستانی
smart	باهوش
child	بچّه
generous/giving	بخشنده
brother	برادر
for	برایِ
to welcome	به جایی خوش آمدن
very well	به خوبی

ح

truly	حقیقتاً

خ

house/home	خانه
fortunately	خوشبختانه

پ

fall/autumn	پاییز / پائیز

د

scientist	دانشمند

tree	درخت
hand	دست
exactly	دقیقاً
again	دوباره
to like/to love	دوست داشتن
yesterday	دیروز

ر

boss	رئیس

س

coin	سکّه
question	سؤال

ش

dinner	شام
strongly	شدیداً
to wash	شستن
to count	شمردن
object	شئ

ع

photographer	عکّاس

ف

tomorrow	فردا
verb	فعل
right away	فوراً

ق

spoon	قاشق
before	قبل از

ک

shoe	کفش
mountain	کوه

ل

please	لطفاً

م

mother	مادر
month/moon	ماه
unfortunately	متأسّفانه
statue	مجسّمه
kindness	محبّت
researcher	محقّق
problem/issue	مسأله
responsible	مسئول
famous	مشهور
teacher	معلّم
guilty	مقصّر
effective	مؤثّر
polite	مؤدّب
politely	مؤدّبانه
important	مهمّ

180

ن

unknown	ناشناخته
painter	نقّاش

و

truly	واقعاً

و

weekly	هفتگی
yet	هنوز

Test Yourself:

9.1 Identify the **Arabic adverbs** from the list of **adverbs** below and rewrite them in the spaces provided. There are 8 **Arabic adverbs** in this exercise.

respectfully   /bă- eh.te.răm/ با احترام

very fast   /tond- tond/ تند تند

right away   /fo.ran/ فوراً

weekly   /haf.te.gi/ هفتگی

please   /lot.fan/ لطفاً

fortunately   /ǩoš.baǩ.tă.ne/ خوشبختانه

exactly   /da.ǧi.ǧan/ دقیقاً

very well   /be- ǩu.bi/ به خوبی

basically   /a.să.san/ اساساً

slowly   /ă.răm/ آرام

entirely   /ta.mă.man/ تماماً

rarely   /be- nod.rat/ به ندرت

possibly   /eh.te.mă.lan/ احتمالاً

yet   /ha.nuz/ هنوز

truly   /ha.ği.ğa.tan/   **حقیقتاً**

tonight   /em.šab/   **امشب**

strongly   /ša.di.dan/   **شدیداً**

yesterday   /di.ruz/   **دیروز**

Example: فوراً   ١–

_____ ٢–

_____ ٣–

_____ ۴–

_____ ۵–

_____ ۶–

_____ ٧–

_____ ٨–

9.2 From the list of the words below, identify the **Arabic words** that carry ع / ٔ /

(hamze) and rewrite the words in the spaces provided. There are 8 words with ع / ٔ /

(hamze) in this exercise.

polite /mo.ʼad.dab/ مُؤدّب

month/moon /măh/ ماه

tomorrow /far.dă/ فردا

celestial /ă.se.mă.ni/ آسمانی

responsible /mas.ʼul/ مَسئول

smart /bă.huš/ باهوش

boss /ra.ʼis/ رَئیس

generous/giving /baǩ.šan.de/ بخشنده

mountain /kuh/ کوه

issue/problem /mas.ʼa.le/ مَسأله

tree /de.raǩt/ درخت

shoe /kafš/ کفش

effective /mo.ʼas.ser/ مُؤثّر

again /do.bă.re/ دوباره

question   /so.'ăl/   **سُؤال**

question   /por.seš/   **پُرسش**

fall/autumn   /pă.'iz/   **پائیز**

spoon   /ğă.šoğ/   **قاشق**

unfortunately   /mo.te.'as.se.fă.ne/   **مُتأسّفانه**

Example: ــــــــــــــ   مُؤدّب   ١-

ــــــــــــــ   ٢-

ــــــــــــــ   ٣-

ــــــــــــــ   ٤-

ــــــــــــــ   ٥-

ــــــــــــــ   ٦-

185

‏ـــــــــــــــــــــ **٧-**

‏ـــــــــــــــــــــ **٨-**

9.3 Look at the transliterations of the words below. Use the information to decide which letter in each word should have a **gemination mark** ّ *(tašdid)*. Underline the letter and then rewrite each word placing the **gemination mark** ّ *(tašdid)* for each word in its appropriate place.

Example: painter   /nağ.ğăš/ ‏نقاش

‏نقّاش

hill   /tap.pe/ ‏تپه

coin   /sek.ke/ ‏سکه

piece /tek.ke/ تکه

photographer /ak.kăs/ عَکاس

researcher /mo.hağ.ğeğ/ محقق

thinking /ta.fak.kor/ تفکر

imagination /ta.ǩay.yol/ تخیل

civilization /ta.mad.don/ تمدن

guilty /mo.ğas.ser/ مقصر

teacher /mo.'al.lem/ معلم

attention /ta.vaj.joh/ توجه

statue /mo.jas.sa.me/ مجسمه

child /bač.če/ بچه

kindness /mo.hab.bat/ محبت

CHAPTER 10

VERBS

فعل ها

/feʻl.hă/

Verbs are usually found at the ends of sentences in Persian. They indicate the occurrence or performance of an action; they may also indicate the existence of a state or condition.

In the Persian language, a conjugated verb contains information about *time* or *tense* (when an action, existence or state of being occurs), *person* (the person or thing speaking, the person or thing spoken to, or the person or thing spoken of) and also, *number* (one or more than one person or thing).

● **The Infinitive Form of Verbs:**

(infinitive) /mas.dar/ مَصدَر

Infinitives carry the main meaning of a verb without showing the time, person and number. In other words, an infinitive is the non-conjugated form of the verb.

Verbs can be divided into the four following groups, based on their structures:

1) Simple Verbs
2) Compound Verbs
3) Prefix Verbs
4) Phrasal Verbs

1) Simple Verbs:
These verbs take the form of only one word.

> **EXAMPLES:**
>
> to see   /di.dan/ دیدن
>
> to go   /raf.tan/ رفتن

2) Compound Verbs:
These verbs take the form of more than one word (a noun or an adjective plus a simple verb).

> **EXAMPLES:**
>
> - a *noun* + a *simple verb*:
>
> to talk   /harf- za.dan/ حرف زدن
>
> to work   /kǎr- kar.dan/ کار کردن
>
> - an *adjective* + a *simple verb*:
>
> to dry   /ǩošk- kar.dan/ خشک کردن
>
> to thank   /ta.šak.kor- kar.dan/ تشکّر کردن

3) Prefix Verbs:
These verbs are made out of a prefix plus a simple verb.

> **EXAMPLES:**
>
> to return   /bar- gaš.tan/ برگشتن
>
> to understand   /dar- yǎf.tan/ دریافتن

4) Phrasal Verbs:
These verbs are made out of a combination of prepositions, prefixes, nouns, adjectives, plus a simple verb.

> **EXAMPLES:**
>
> to stop working /az- kǎr- of.tǎ.dan/ از کار افتادن
>
> to step forward   /pǎ- piš- go.zǎš.tan/ پا پیش گذاشتن
>
> **Note:**
>
> In the Persian language, all infinitives end in تَن /.tan/, or in دَن /.dan/ - یدَن /i.dan/.

● **Verb Tenses:**

/za.măn.hă.ye- fe'l/ زمان های فعل

These are the forms of the verb that indicate "time". There are 11 common verb tenses in the Persian language:

1) Simple Present   2) Present Subjunctive   3) Present Progressive   4) Simple Past
5) Imperfect Indicative   6) Present Perfect   7) Past Perfect   8) Past Subjunctive
9) Past Progressive   10) Simple Future   11) Command

1) Simple Present

Personal Suffix + Present Stem + Tense Prefix (می)

It is used to indicate one of the following:

a)   An action at the present time.

EXAMPLES:

رایان پیشنهاد تو را می پذیرد.

/ră.yăn- piš.na.hă.de- to- ră- mi.pa.zi.rad/
Ryan accepts your suggestion.

من در را باز می کنم.

/man- dar- ră- băz- mi.ko.nam/
I open the door.

b)   A habitual action.

EXAMPLES:

شما هر روز با هم می رقصید؟

/šo.mă- har- ruz- bă- ham- mi.rağ.sid/
Do you dance together every day?

من هر شب چای سبز می نوشم.

/man- har- šab- čă.ye- sabz- mi.nu.šam/
I drink green tea every night.

c)   An action in the future.

EXAMPLES:

برادرم فردا به اُروپا می رود.

/ba.ră.da.ram- far.dă- be- o.ru.pă- mi.ra.vad/
My brother will go to Europe tomorrow.

من سال آینده دکتر می شوم.

/man- să.le- ă.yan.de- dok̅.tor- mi.ša.vam/

I will become a doctor next year.

2) Present Subjunctive

Personal Suffix + Present Stem + Tense Prefix (بـ)

It is used after a verb that expresses one of the following:

   a) A suggestion.

EXAMPLES:

توصیه می کنیم که با ما بیایی.

/to.si.ye- mi.ko.nim- ke- bă- mă- bi.yă.yi/

[we] recommend that [you] come with us.

پیشنهاد می کنم که با بانک تماس بگیرید.

/piš.na.hăd- mi.ko.nam- ke- bă- bănk- ta.măs- be.gi.rid/

[I] suggest that [you] contact the bank.

   b) A wish.

EXAMPLES:

مادرم امیدوار است که تو به دیدنش بروی.

/mă.da.ram- o.mid.văr- ast- ke- to- be- di.da.naš- be.ra.vi/

My mother is hoping that you go to see her.

دلم می خواهد صدای دخترم را بشنوی.

/de.lam- mi.k̅ă.had- se̅.dă.ye- dok̅.ta.ram- ră- be.še.na.vi/

[I] would like [you] to hear my daughter's voice.

   c) A preference.

EXAMPLES:

لیلا ترجیح می دهد که پسرش زود بخوابد.

/ley.lă- tar.jih- mi.da.had- ke- pe.sa.raš- zud- be.k̅ă.bad/

Leila prefers that her son go to sleep early.

آنها ترجیح می دهند که با ما سفر کنند.

/ăn.hă- tar.jih- mi.da.hand- ke- bă- mă- sa.far- ko.nand/

They prefer to travel with us.

192

d) A doubt.

EXAMPLES:

شک دارم آنها حقیقت را به دوستانشان بگویند.

/šak- dǎ.ram- ǎn.hǎ- ha.ǧi.ǧat- rǎ- be- dus.tǎ.ne.šǎn- be.gu.yand/

[I] doubt that they <u>tell</u> their friends the truth.

بعید است دوستانت بیایند.

/ba.ʿid- ast- dus.tǎ.nat- bi.yǎ.yand/

It is unlikely that your friends will <u>come</u>.

e) A necessity.

EXAMPLES:

من احتیاج دارم دست هایم را بشویم.

/man- eh.ti.yǎj- dǎ.ram- dast.hǎ.yam- rǎ- be.šu.yam/

I need to <u>wash</u> my hands.

لازم است به خانه ی سارا برویم.

/lǎ.zem- ast- be- ǩǎ.ne.ye- sǎ.rǎ- be.ra.vim/

It is necessary that we <u>go</u> to Sara's house.

3) Present Progressive

Personal Suffix + Present Stem +Tense Prefix (می) + Present Tense of Auxiliary Verb (داشتن)

This tense describes an action that is happening right now and is on-going. The simple present tense of the verb "داشتن" /dǎš.tan/ is always used as an auxiliary verb with the main verb in this tense.

EXAMPLES:

لیلا دارد با برادرت حرف می زند.

/ley.lǎ- dǎ.rad- bǎ- ba.rǎ.da.rat- harf- mi.za.nad/

Leila <u>is talking</u> to your brother.

من دارم به آهنگ تو گوش می دهم.

/man- dǎ.ram- be- ǎ.han.ge- to- guš- mi.da.ham/

I <u>am listening</u> to your song.

4) Simple Past

Personal Suffix + Present Stem + Tense Prefix (می)

It is used to express an action that happened in the past and was completed.

EXAMPLES:

سام کلید خانه اش را به من داد.

/săm- ke.li.de- kă.ne.aš- ră- be- man- dăd/
Sam <u>gave</u> me the key to his house.

من دیروز به لیلا تلفن زدم.

/man- di.ruz- be- ley.lă- te.le.fon- za.dam/
I <u>called</u> Leila yesterday.

5) Imperfect Indicative

Personal Suffix + Past Stem + Tense Prefix (می)

(The English equivalent: *simple past* or *past progressive* or *"used to"* + *infinitive*)

This tense is used to express an action representing one of the following scenarios:

    a) An action that was continuous in the past.

EXAMPLES:

من قبلاً ماشین می فروختم.

/man- ğab.lan- mă.šin- mi.fo.ruk.tam/
I <u>used to sell</u> cars.

بعد از مهمانی، تا سه روز دستم درد می کرد.

/ba'd- az- meh.mă.ni- tă- se- ruz- das.tam- dard- mi.kard/
After the party, my hand <u>hurt</u> for three days.

    b) An action that was done by someone habitually (for a short or long period of time) in the past.

EXAMPLES:

وقتی در لندن بودم، خیلی به آن پارک می رفتم.

/vağ.ti- dar- lan.dan- bu.dam- key.li- be- ăn- părk- mi.raf.tam/
When [I] was in London, [I] <u>went</u> to that park a lot.

وقتی جوان تر بودم، از خرید بدم می آمد.

/vağ.ti- ja.văn.tar- bu.dam- az- ka.rid- ba.dam- mi.ă.mad/
When [I] was younger, [I] <u>hated</u> shopping.

c) An action that was in progress at some point in the past (even for a very short amount of time).

EXAMPLES:

وقتی از کنار اتاقش رَد می شدم، گریه اش را شنیدم.

/vağ.ti- az- ke.nă.re- o.tă.ğaš- rad- mi.šo.dam- ger.ye.aš- ră- še.ni.dam/

When [I] was passing by her room, [I] heard her crying.

میزش را که تمیز می کردم، عکس تو را پیدا کردم.

/mi.zaš- ră- ke- ta.miz- mi.kar.dam- ak.se- to- ră- pey.dă- kar.dam/

[I] was cleaning his/her desk, when [I] found your picture.

6) Present Perfect

Present Tense of Auxiliary Verb (بودن) + Past Participle

(The English equivalent: present perfect or past progressive)

This tense is used to express an action that has happened in the past, but the effect or result of which continues to the present time.

EXAMPLES:

لیلا مشق هایش را تمام کرده است.

/ley.lă- mašğ.hă.yaš- ră- ta.măm- kar.de- ast/

Leila has finished her homework.

سارا دورتا دور دنیا سفر کرده است.

/să.ră- dor.tă.do.re- don.yă- sa.far- kar.de- ast/

Sara has traveled all around the world.

گربه کنار پنجره خوابیده است.

/gor.be- ke.nă.re- pan.je.re- kă.bi.de- ast/

The cat is sleeping next to the window.

خواهرهایت آنجا نشسته اند.

/kă.har.hă.yat- ăn.jă- ne.šas.te.and/

Your sisters are sitting there.

7) Past Perfect

Past Tense of Auxiliary Verb (بودن) + Past Participle

This tense is used to express an action that took place in the past before another past action.

195

EXAMPLES:

قبل از اینکه به کانادا بیایم، برف ندیده بودم.

/ğabl- az- in.ke- be- kă.nă.dă- bi.yă.yam- barf- na.di.de- bu.dam/
[I] <u>hadn't seen</u> the snow before [I] came to Canada.

قول داده بودند که می آیند، امّا نیامدند.

/ğol- dă.de- bu.dand- ke- mi.ă.yand- am.mă- na.yă.ma.dand/
[They] <u>had promised</u> to come, but [they] didn't.

8) Past Subjunctive

Present Subjunctive of Auxiliary Verb (بودن) + Past Participle

This tense is used to express an action that might have happened in the past.

EXAMPLES:

ممکن است رایان ماشینش را فروخته باشد.

/mom.ken- ast- ră.yăn- mă.ši.naš- ră- fo.ruǩ.te- bă.šad/
Ryan <u>might have sold</u> his car.

شاید دوستانت از سفر برگشته باشند.

/šă.yad- dus.tă.nat- az- sa.far- bar.gaš.te- bă.šand/
Your friends <u>might have come back</u> from the trip.

9) Past Progressive

Personal Suffix + Past Stem + Tense Prefix (می) + Past Tense of Auxiliary Verb (داشتن)

This tense is used to describe an action that was in progress at some point in the past. The simple past tense of the verb "داشتن" /dăš.tan/ is always used (as an auxiliary verb) with the main verb in this tense.

EXAMPLES:

داشتم شام می پختم که دخترم به خانه آمد.

/dăš.tam- šăm- mi.poǩ.tam- ke- doǩ.ta.ram- be- ǩă.ne- ă.mad/
[I] <u>was cooking</u> dinner when my daughter came home.

وقتی داشتم در پارک قدم می زدم، سگّت را دیدم.

/vağ.ti- dăš.tam- dar- părk- ğa.dam- mi.za.dam- sa.gat- ră- di.dam/
When [I] <u>was walking</u> in the park, [I] saw your dog.

196

10) Simple Future

Past Stem + Present Subjunctive (w/o prefix بِ) of Auxiliary Verb (خواستن)

This tense is used to express an action that will take place at some point in time in the future. The present subjunctive tense of the verb "خواستن" /kǎs.tan/ without the prefix بِ /be/ is always used (as an auxiliary verb) with the main verb in this tense.

EXAMPLES:

بچّه ها باز هم به دیدنَت خواهند آمد.

/bač.če.hǎ- bǎz- ham- be- di.da.nat- kǎ.hand- ǎ.mad/
The children will come to visit you again.

سارا تو را خواهد بخشید.

/sǎ.rǎ- to- rǎ- kǎ.had- bak.šid/
Sara will forgive you.

11) Command

Personal Suffix + Present Stem + Tense Prefix (بِ)

This tense is used to express an action that is one of the following:

a) a command.

EXAMPLES:

همین الآن به خانه برگرد!

/ha.min- al.ǎn- be- kǎ.ne- bar.gard/
Come back home right now!

ساکت باشید!

/sǎ.ket- bǎ.šid/
Be quiet!

b) a request.

EXAMPLES:

حقیقت را بپذیرید!

/ha.ği.ğat- rǎ- be.pa.zi.rid/
Accept the truth!

حرفم را باور کن!

/har.fam- rǎ- bǎ.var- kon/

<u>Believe</u> me!

Note:

For the *command* form of the verb, the use of prefix بـ /be/ depends on the verb. For some verbs this prefix بـ /be/ could be eliminated, especially when they are *compound verbs*, *prefix verbs* and *phrasal verbs*.

EXAMPLES:

- *compound verbs*:

در را باز کن!

/dar- rǎ- bǎz- kon/

<u>Open</u> the door!

- *prefix verbs*:

کتاب را بردار!

/ke.tǎb- rǎ- bar.dǎr/

<u>Pick up</u> the book!

- *phrasal verbs*:

این بلوز را به تن کن!

/in- bo.luz- rǎ- be- tan- kon/

<u>Put</u> this shirt <u>on</u>!

- ### Elements of a Simple Verb:

A conjugated simple verb is formed by three elements:

1) Tense Prefixes

پیشوَندِ فعل /piš.van.de- fe'l/

2) Present Stems or Past Stems

بُنِ مُضارِع – بُنِ ماضی /bo.ne- mo.zǎ.re'/ - /bo.ne- mǎ.zi/

198

3) Personal Suffixes (Endings)

/še.nă.se/ شناسه

1) *Tense Prefixes*:
Tense prefixes are added to the beginnings of *simple verbs*. Conjugated verbs may start with the prefixes می /mi/ or بـ /be/ or may start without a prefix.

EXAMPLES:

- *tense prefix* می /mi/ :

I understand. /mi.fah.mam/ می فهمَم

- *tense prefix* بـ /be/ :

I might understand. /be.fah.mam/ بـِفهمَم

- without a *tense prefix* :

He/She understood. /fah.mid/ فهمید

    a) The prefix می /mi/ is used in the conjugation of these tenses: *simple present*, *present progressive*, *imperfect indicative* and *past progressive*.

    b) The prefix بـ /be/ is used in the conjugation of these tenses: *present subjunctive* and *command*.

    c) There is no tense prefix for the following tenses: *simple past*, *present perfect*, *past perfect*, *past subjunctive* and *simple future*.

    Note:
Some *command tenses* do not use a *tense prefix*.

2) *Present Stems* or *Past Stems*:
The part of a verb that contains the main meaning is called the *"stem"*. In "regular" verbs, the *present stem* does not change despite the conjugation. In "irregular" verbs, the *present stem* of the verb changes when the verb is conjugated.

EXAMPLES:

- for *present stem*:

to understand /fahm/ فَهم (فَهمیدَن)

- for *past stem*:

to understand   /fah.mid/   فَهمید (فَهمیدَن)

3) *Personal Suffixes (Endings)*:

This part shows the person and number being spoken of by the verb. In the Persian language, conjugated verbs show both the *person* and the *number* through *personal suffixes (endings)*. There are six *personal suffixes*, out of which three are *singular*, and three are *plural*:

(I)   /am/   مَ

(You *sing.*)   /i/   ی

(He/She)   /ad/   دَ

(We)   /im/   یم

(You *pl.*)   /id/   ید

(They)   /and/   نَد

EXAMPLES:

- singular:

I understand.   /mi.fah.mam/   می فهمَم

You *sing.* understand.   /mi.fah.mi/   می فهمی

He/She understands.   /mi.fah.mad/   می فهمَد

- plural:

We understand.   /mi.fah.mim/   می فهمیم

You *pl.* understand.   /mi.fah.mid/   می فهمید

They understand.   /mi.fah.mand/   می فهمَند

Note:

Conjugated verbs in specific tenses might not carry a *personal suffix (ending)*.

200

EXAMPLES:

He/She understood.   /fah.mid/ فهمید

Note:

When the *tense prefix* بـ /be/ is added to the beginning of a verb that starts with the letter آ /ǎ/ , the *tense prefix* بـ /be/ changes into بیـ /bi/ and the letter آ /ǎ/ turns into ا /ǎ/.

EXAMPLES:

to come   /ǎ.ma.dan/ آمَدن

↓

I might come.   /bi.yǎ.yam/ بیایَم

Note:

When the *tense prefix* بـ /be/ is added to the beginning of a verb that starts with any of the three following vowels, the *tense prefix* بـ /be/ turns into بیـ /bi/ and the vowels also have orthographical changes:

- ‑ اُ /o/ ⟶ ُ /o/
- ‑ آ /a/ ⟶ ´ /a/
- ‑ ا /e/ ⟶ /e/

EXAMPLES:

to fall   /of.tǎ.dan/ اُفتادن

↓

I might fall.   /bi.yof.tam/ بیُفتم

to increase   /af.zu.dan/ أفزودن

↓

I might increase.   /bi.yaf.zǎ.yam/ بیَفزایم

201

to presume   /en.găš.tan/ اِنگاشتن

↓

I might presume.   /bi.yen.gă.ram/ بینگارم

- **Regular and Irregular Verbs:**

Verbs may also be classified as either *"regular"* or *"irregular"* based on the way they conjugate in the present tense:

1) Regular Verbs:
The conjugation of these verbs is regular, which means that the *present stem* of these verbs does not change when the verb is conjugated.

EXAMPLES:

to bring   /ă.var.dan/ آوَردَن

to make someone laugh   /ǩan.dăn.dan/ خَنداندَن

2) Irregular Verbs:
The conjugation of these verbs is irregular, which means the *present stem* of these verbs will change when the verb is conjugated.

EXAMPLES:

to see   /di.dan/ دیدَن

to tell/ to say   /gof.tan/ گُفتَن

Note:

Most Persian verbs ending in "تَن" /.tan/ are "irregular".

- **Stems of the Verb:**

/bon.hă.ye- fe'l/   بُن های فعل

These are the parts of a verb that contain the main meaning of that verb. There are two types of *stems*: *present stems* and *past stems*.

202

- Present Stems of Regular Verbs:

There are rules for identifying the **present stems** of **regular verbs**.

a) Present stems of *regular verbs* (infinitives) ending in " تَن " /.tan/ are formed by eliminating the " تَن " /.tan/ from the end of the infinitives.

EXAMPLES:

to bloom   /še.kof.tan/ = /še.kof/ شکُفَ = شِکُفتَن

to kill   /koš.tan/ = /koš/ کُش = کُشتَن

b) Present stems of *regular verbs* (infinitives) ending in " دَن " /.dan/ or " یدَن " /i.dan/ are formed by eliminating the " دَن " /.dan/ or " یدَن " /i.dan/ from the end of the infinitives.

EXAMPLES:

- verbs (infinitives) ending in " دَن " /.dan/:

to eat   /ǩor.dan/ = /ǩor/   خور = خوردَن

to read   /ǩǎn.dan/ = /ǩǎn/ خوان = خوانـدَن

- verbs (infinitives) ending in " یدَن " /i.dan/:

to sleep   /ǩǎ.bi.dan/ = /ǩǎb/ خواب = خوابیدَن

to jump   /pa.ri.dan/ = /par/ پَر = پَریدَن

203

- **Present Stems of Irregular Verbs:**

> **Present stems** of **irregular verbs** change when the verb is conjugated, therefore, there is no simple way to establish a rule. The table below shows the *present stems* of some common *irregular verbs*.

Present Stem of Irregular Verbs
(Table 10.1)

definition	present stem	infinitive
to come	آی /ăy/	آمدن /ă.ma.dan/
to fall	افت /oft/	افتادن /of.tă.dan/
to stand	ایست /ist/	ایستادن /is.tă.dan/
to pick up	بردار /bar.dăr/	برداشتن /bar.dăš.tan/
to return	برگرد /bar.gard/	برگشتن /bar.gaš.tan/
to close	بند /band/	بستن /bas.tan/
to be	باش /bă/	بودن /bu.dan/
to cook	پز /paz/	پختن /poǩ.tan/
to be able to	توان /ta.văn/	توانستن /ta.vă.nes.tan/
to want	خواه /ǩăh/	خواستن /ǩăs.tan/

to give	ده	دادن
	/deh/	/dă.dan/
to have	دار	داشتن
	/dăr/	/dăš.tan/
to know	دان	دانستن
	/dăn/	/dă.nes.tan/
to see	بین	دیدن
	/bin/	/di.dan/
to go	رو	رَفتن
	/ro/	/raf.tan/
to build	ساز	ساختن
	/săz/	/săǩ.tan/
to become	شو	شدن
	/šo/	/šo.dan/
to wash	شوی	شستن
	/šuy/	/šos.tan/
to break	شکن	شکستن
	/še.kan/	/še.kas.tan/
to recognize	شناس	شناختن
	/še.năs/	/še.năǩ.tan/
to hear	شنو	شنیدن
	/še.no/	/še.ni.dan/
to send	فرست	فرستادن
	/fe.rest/	/fe.res.tă.dan/
to sell	فروش	فروختن
	/fo.ruš/	/fo.ruǩ.tan/
to do	کن	کردن
	/kon/	/kar.dan/

to put	گذار	گذاشتن
	/go.zăr/	/go.zăš.tan/
to catch	گیر	گرفتن
	/gir/	/ge.ref.tan/
to tell	گوی	گفتن
	/guy/	/gof.tan/
to sit	نشین	نشستن
	/ne.šin/	/ne.šas.tan/
to write	نویس	نوشتن
	/ne.vis/	/ne.veš.tan/

- Past Stems of Regular Verbs:

There are rules for identifying the **past stems** of **regular verbs**:

a) Past stems of *regular verbs* (infinitives) ending in "تَن" /.tan/ are formed by

eliminating the "نَ" /an/ from the end of the infinitives.

EXAMPLES:

to bloom   /še.kof.tan/ = /še.koft/ شكُفت = شِكُفتَن

to kill   /koš.tan/ = /košt/ كُشت = كُشتَن

b) Past stems of *regular verbs* (infinitives) ending in "دَن" /.dan/ or "یدَن"

/i.dan/ are formed by eliminating the "نَ" /an/ from the end of the infinitives.

EXAMPLES:

- verbs (infinitives) ending in "دَن" /.dan/:

to eat   /ǩor.dan/ = /ǩord/ خوردَن = خورد

to read   /ǩăn.dan/ = /ǩănd/ خواندَن = خواند

- verbs (infinitives) ending in " یدَن " /i.dan/:

to sleep   /kǎ.bi.d<s>an</s>/ = /kǎ.bid/   خوابیدَن = خوابید

to jump   /pa.ri.d<s>an</s>/ = /pa.rid/   پَریدَن = پَرید

- Past Stems of Irregular Verbs:

There are rules for identifying the **past stems** of **irregular verbs**:

a) Past stems of *irregular verbs* (infinitives) ending in " تَن " /.tan/ are formed by

eliminating the " ن ' " /an/ from the end of the infinitives.

EXAMPLES:

to say/to tell   /gof.t<s>an</s>/ = /goft/   گُفتَن = گُفت

to break   /še.kas.t<s>an</s>/ = /še.kast/   شِکَستَن = شِکَست

b) Past stems of *irregular verbs* (infinitives) ending in " دَن " /.dan/ or " یدَن "

/i.dan/ are formed by eliminating the " ن ' " /an/ from the end of the infinitives.

EXAMPLES:

- verbs (infinitives) ending in " دَن " /.dan/:

to come   /ǎ.ma.d<s>an</s>/ = /ǎ.mad/   آمَدَن = آمَد

to fall   /of.tǎ.d<s>an</s>/ = /of.tǎd/   اُفتادَن = اُفتاد

- verbs (infinitives) ending in " یدَن " /i.dan/:

to create   /ǎ.fa.ri.d<s>an</s>/ = /ǎ.fa.rid/   آفَریدَن = آفَرید

to choose   /bar.go.zi.d<s>an</s>/ = /bar.go.zid/   بَرگُزیدَن = بَرگُزید

Note:
The rules to identify **past stems** of both *regular verbs* and *irregular verbs* are the same.

● **Past Participles:**

In the Persian language, the *past participles* are called *"objective adjectives"* and are formed by:

> (past stem of the verb + suffix ه — ـه /e/ .)

EXAMPLES:

done   /kar.de/   کَرده = ه + کَرد

seen   /di.de/   دیده = ه + دید

told   /gof.te/   گُفته = ه + گُفت

● **Auxiliary Verb:**

/fe'.le- ko.ma.ki/   فعل کُمَکی

To form some tenses, the use of an *auxiliary verb* beside the main verb is needed. The most common Persian *auxiliary verbs* used in forming the tenses are:

> to be   /bu.dan/   بودَن
>
> to want   /ǩǎs.tan/   خواستَن
>
> to have   /dǎš.tan/   داشتَن
>
> to become   /šo.dan/   شُدَن

EXAMPLES:

- for the *auxiliary verb*: /bu.dan/   بودَن

آنها به اُروپا رفته بودند.

/ǎn.hǎ- be- o.ru.pǎ- raf.te- bu.dand/
They <u>had</u> gone to Europe.

آنها به اُروپا رفته اند.

/ǎn.hǎ- be- o.ru.pǎ- raf.te.and/
They <u>have</u> gone to Europe.

- for the *auxiliary verb*: /ǩǎs.tan/   خواستَن

من خواهَم فهمید.

/man- ǩǎ.ham- fah.mid/

I <u>will</u> understand.

- for the *auxiliary verb*: /dǎš.tan/ داشتَن

من دارَم روزنامه می خوانم.

/man- dǎ.ram- ruz.nǎ.me- mi.ǩǎ.nam/

I <u>am</u> read<u>ing</u> the newspaper.

من داشتم روزنامه می خواندم.

/man- dǎš.tam- ruz.nǎ.me- mi.ǩǎn.dam/

I <u>was</u> read<u>ing</u> the newspaper.

- for the *auxiliary verb*: /šo.dan/ شُدَن

هوا بهتر می شَود.

/ha.vǎ- beh.tar- mi.ša.vad/

The weather <u>gets</u> better.

هوا بهتر شُد.

/ha.vǎ- beh.tar- šod/

The weather <u>got</u> better.

In the table below, the full conjugation of the verb (to do) /kar.dan/ کَردَن in the most common eleven tenses of the Persian language has been provided.

Full Conjugation of the verb کردن in the Most Common Eleven Tenses
(Table 10.2)

		Structure of the Verb in Simple Present Tense (to do) /kar.dan/ کَردَن Personal Suffix + Present Stem + Tense Prefix (می)	
می + کُن + یم می کُنیم /mi.ko.nim/	ما	می + کُن + َم می کُنَم /mi.ko.nam/	من
می + کُن + ید می کُنید /mi.ko.nid/	شما	می + کُن + ی می کُنی /mi.ko.ni/	تو
می + کُن + َند می کُنَند /mi.ko.nand/	آنها/ ایشان	می + کُن + َد می کُنَد /mi.ko.nad/	او

Structure of the Verb in
Present Subjunctive Tense

(to do) /kar.dan/ کَردَن

Personal Suffix + Present Stem + Tense Prefix (ـبِ)

بـِ + کُن + یم بِکُنیم /be.ko.nim/	ما	بـِ + کُن + مَ بِکُنَم /be.ko.nam/	من
بـِ + کُن + ید بِکُنید /be.ko.nid/	شما	بـِ + کُن + ی بِکُنی /be.ko.ni/	تو
بـِ + کُن + ند بِکُنَند /be.ko.nand/	آنها/ ایشان	بـِ + کُن + دَ بِکُنَد /be.ko.nad/	او

Structure of the Verb in Present Progressive Tense

کَردَن /kar.dan/ (to do)

Personal Suffix + Present Stem + Tense Prefix (می) + Present Tense of Auxiliary Verb (داشتن)

داریم + می + کُن + یم داریم می کُنیم /dă.rim- mi.ko.nim/	ما	دارَم + می + کُن + َم دارَم می کُنَم /dă.ram- mi.ko.nam/	من
دارید + می + کُن + ید دارید می کُنید /dă.rid- mi.ko.nid/	شما	داری + می + کُن + ی داری می کُنی /dă.ri- mi.ko.ni/	تو
دارَند + می + کُن + َند دارَند می کُنَند /dă.rand- mi.ko.nand/	آنها/ ایشان	دارَد + می + کُن + َد دارَد می کُنَد /dă.rad- mi.ko.nad/	او

Structure of the Verb in Simple Past Tense كَردَن /kar.dan/ (to do) Personal Suffix + Past Stem					
گَرد + یم گَردیم /kar.dim/	ما	گَرد +َم گَردَم /kar.dam/	من
گَرد + ید گَردید /kar.did/	شما	گَرد + ی گَردی /kar.di/	تو
گَرد + َند گَردَند /kar.dand/	آنها/ ایشان	گَرد + – گَرد /kard/	او

Structure of the Verb in Imperfect Indicative Tense		
(to do) /kar.dan/ گَردَن			
Personal Suffix + Past Stem + Tense Prefix (می)			
می + گَرد + یم می گَردیم /mi.kar.dim/	ما	می + گَرد +َم می گَردَم /mi.kar.dam/	من
می + گَرد + ید می گَردید /mi.kar.did/	شما	می + گَرد + ی می گَردی /mi.kar.di/	تو
می + گَرد +َند می گَردَند /mi.kar.dand/	آنها/ ایشان	می + گَرد + – می گَرد /mi.kard/	او

	Structure of the Verb in Present Perfect Tense گَردَن /kar.dan/ (to do) Present Tense of Auxiliary Verb (بودن) + Past Participle			
گَرده + ایم گَرده ایم /kar.de- im/	ما	گَرده + ام گَرده ام /kar.de.am/		من
گَرده + اید گَرده اید /kar.de.id/	شما	گَرده + ای گَرده ای /kar.de.i/		تو
گَرده + اند گَرده اند /kar.de.and/	آنها/ ایشان	گَرده + است گَرده است /kar.de- ast/		او

<table>
<tr><td colspan="5" align="center">Structure of the Verb in
Past Perfect Tense

(to do) /kar.dan/   گَردَن

Past Tense of Auxiliary Verb (بودن) + Past Participle</td></tr>
<tr>
<td align="center">گَرده + بودیم

گَرده بودیم

/bu.dim/ + past participle</td>
<td align="center">ما</td>
<td align="center">گَرده + بودَم

گَرده بودَم

/bu.dam/ + past participle</td>
<td align="center">من</td>
</tr>
<tr>
<td align="center">گَرده + بودید

گَرده بودید

/bu.did/ + past participle</td>
<td align="center">شما</td>
<td align="center">گَرده + بودی

گَرده بودی

/bu.di/ + past participle</td>
<td align="center">تو</td>
</tr>
<tr>
<td align="center">گَرده + بودَند

گَرده بودَند

/bu.dand/ + past participle</td>
<td align="center">آنها/
ایشان</td>
<td align="center">گَرده + بود

گَرده بود

/bud/ + past participle</td>
<td align="center">او</td>
</tr>
</table>

216

Structure of the Verb in Past Subjunctive Tense (to do) /kar.dan/ کَردَن Present Subjunctive of Auxiliary Verb (بودن) + Past Participle				
گَرده + باشیم گَرده باشیم /kar.de- bǎ.šim/	ما	گَرده + باشَم گَرده باشَم /kar.de- bǎ.šam/	من
گَرده + باشید گَرده باشید /kar.de- bǎ.šid/	شما	گَرده + باشی گَرده باشی /kar.de- bǎ.ši/	تو
گَرده + باشَند گَرده باشَند /kar.de- bǎ.šand/	آنها/ ایشان	گَرده + باشَد گَرده باشَد /kar.de- bǎ.šad/	او

VERBS

Structure of the Verb in
Past Progressive Tense

گَردَن /kar.dan/ (to do)

Personal Suffix + Past Stem + Tense Prefix (می) + Past Tense of Auxiliary Verb (داشتن)

داشتیم + می + گَرد + یم داشتیم می گَردیم /dăš.tim- mi.kar.dim/	ما	داشتم + می + گَرد + َم داشتَم می گَردَم /dăš.tam- mi.kar.dam/	من
داشتید + می + گَرد + ید داشتید می گَردید /dăš.tid- mi.kar.did/	شما	داشتی + می + گَرد + ی داشتی می گَردی /dăš.ti- mi.kar.di/	تو
داشتند + می + گَرد + َند داشتَند می گَردَند /dăš.tand- mi.kar.dand/	آنها/ ایشان	داشت + می + گَرد + – داشت می گَرد /dăšt- mi.kard/	او

	Structure of the Verb in Simple Future Tense گَردَن /kar.dan/ (to do) Past Stem + Present Subjunctive (w/o prefix بِ) of Auxiliary Verb (خواستن)		
خواهیم + گَرد خواهیم گَرد /ǩǎ.him- kard/	ما	خواهَم + گَرد خواهَم گَرد /ǩǎ.ham- kard/	من
خواهید + گَرد خواهید گَرد /ǩǎ.hid- kard/	شما	خواهی + گَرد خواهی گَرد /ǩǎ.hi- kard/	تو
خواهَند + گَرد خواهَند گَرد /ǩǎ.hand- kard/	آنها/ ایشان	خواهَد + گَرد خواهَد گَرد /ǩǎ.had- kard/	او

<table>
<tr><td colspan="5" align="center">Structure of the Verb in
Command Tense

(to do) /kar.dan/ کَردَن

Personal Suffix + Present Stem + Tense Prefix (بِ)</td></tr>
<tr>
<td align="center">بِ + کُن + ید
بِکُنید
/be.ko.nid/</td>
<td align="center">شما</td>
<td align="center">بِ + کُن + –
بِکُن
/be.kon/</td>
<td align="center">تو</td>
</tr>
</table>

● **Transitive Verbs and Intransitive Verbs:**

Verbs may also be classified as either *transitive* or *intransitive*.

- Transitive Verbs:

These verbs require at least one *object* in the sentence.

EXAMPLES:

من پنجره را بستم.

/man- pan.je.re- rǎ- bas.tam/
I <u>closed</u> the window.

ما بچّه ها را خنداندیم.

/mǎ- bač.če.hǎ- rǎ- ǩan.dǎn.dim/
We <u>made</u> the children <u>laugh</u>.

- Intransitive Verbs:

These verbs do not require an *object* in the sentence.

220

EXAMPLES:

سارا نشست.

/sǎ.rǎ- ne.šast/

Sara <u>sat down</u>.

بچّه دارد می خوابد.

/bač.če- dǎ.rad- mi.ǩǎ.bad/

The child <u>is sleeping</u>.

- **Dual-mood Verbs:**

Dual-mood verbs are verbs that could be both *transitive* and *intransitive*.

EXAMPLES:

- for *intransitive*:

فنجانِ من شکست.

/fen.jǎ.ne- man- še.kast/

My cup <u>broke</u>.

- for *transitive*:

رایان فنجانِ من را شکست.

/rǎ.yǎn- fen.jǎ.ne- man- rǎ- še.kast/

Ryan <u>broke</u> my cup.

- for *intransitive*:

آب ریخت.

/ǎb- riǩt/

The water <u>spilled</u>.

- for *transitive*:

من آب را ریختم.

/man- ǎb- rǎ- riǩ.tam/

I <u>spilled</u> the water.

- **Active and Passive Voices:**

Verbs can have an *active* or *passive* voice.

221

- Active Voice:

This is when the *subject* is known.

EXAMPLES:

- *subject*: سارا

سارا نامه را نوشت.

/săm- nă.me- ră- ne.vešt/
Sam <u>wrote</u> the letter.

- *subject*: من

من سیب را خوردم.

/man- sib-ră- ǩor.dam/
I <u>ate</u> the apple.

- Passive Voice:

This is when the *subject* is unknown.

EXAMPLES:

نامه نوشته شد.

/nă.me- ne.veš.te- šod/
The letter <u>was written</u>.

سیب خورده شد.

/sib- ǩor.de- šod/
The apple <u>was eaten</u>.

To change a verb from its *active* to *passive* voice, we have to:

a) eliminate the *subject* and replace it with the *object*.

b) eliminate the *direct object indicator*: را /ră/ .

c) replace the *main verb* with its *past participle* (objective adjective).

d) conjugate the *auxiliary verb* شُدَن /šo.dan/ in the same tense as the main

verb (in its *active* voice) to match the *person* and *number* of the *object* and add it to the *past participle*.

EXAMPLES:

- *active* voice:

من سام را دیدم.

/man- săm- ră- di.dam/
I <u>saw</u> Sam.

- *passive* voice:

سام دیده شد.

/săm- di.de- šod/
Sam <u>was seen</u>.

Keep in Mind: *Intransitive verbs* do not have a *passive* voice.

- **Negative Verbs:**

Negative verbs are the verbs that indicate the lack of occurrence or performance of an action, or the existence of a state or condition. Almost all types of verbs could be changed into a *negative verb* by adding the prefix نَ /na/ or نِ /ne/ to the beginning of the *main verb*.

EXAMPLES:

- *positive* form:

I run. /mi.da.vam/ می دوم.

- *negative* form:

I do not run. /ne.mi.da.vam/ نِ + می دوم = نِمی دوم.

- *positive* form:

I ran. /da.vi.dam/ دویدم.

- *negative* form:

I did not run. /na.da.vi.dam/ نَ + دویدم = نَدویدم.

223

- There are two **"exceptions"** to the above rule:

a) In the *future tense*, we conjugate the auxiliary verb; therefore, the prefix نَ /na/ will be added to the beginning of the *auxiliary verb* خواستن /ĸăs.tan/ to form the *negative verb*.

EXAMPLES:

- *positive* form:

I will go.   /ĸă.ham- raft/   خواهم رفت.

- *negative* form:

I will not go.   /na.ĸă.ham- raft/ نَخواهم رفت = نَ + خواهم رفت

b) In the *present subjunctive tense* the prefix نَ /na/ will "replace" the prefix بِ /be/ to form the *negative verb*.

EXAMPLES:

- *positive*:

[I] might go. /šă.yad- be.ra.vam/ شاید بِروم.

- *negative*:

[I] might not go. /šă.yad- na.ra.vam/ شاید نَروم = روم + نَ + شاید

Note:

Because verbs in the *present progressive* and *past progressive* indicate the continuation of performing an action, the negative forms of these tenses do not make sense in the Persian language. Therefore, the negative form of these two tenses in Persian would be the *simple present tense* and the *imperfect indicative tense*.

EXAMPLES:

- *positive* form (*past progressive tense*):

وقتی آمدی، داشتم لباس هایم را می شستم.

/vağ.ti- ă.ma.di- dăš.tam- le.băs.hă.yam- ră- mi.šos.tam/
I <u>was washing</u> my clothes when you came.

- *negative* form (*imperfect indicative tense*):

وقتی آمدی، لباس هایم را نمی شستم.

/vağ.ti- ă.ma.di- le.băs.hă.yam- ră- ne.mi.šos.tam/
I <u>was not washing</u> my clothes when you came.

- *positive* form *(present progressive tense)*:

الآن دارم با یک نفر <u>صحبت می کنم</u>.

/al.ăn- dă.ram- bă- yek- na.far- soh.bat- mi.ko.nam/
I <u>am talking</u> to someone right now.

- *negative* form *(simple present tense)*:

الآن با هیچکس <u>صحبت نمی کنم</u>.

/al.ăn- bă- hič.kas- soh.bat- ne.mi.ko.nam/
I <u>am not talking</u> to anyone right now.

Note:

To change a *command* into its *negative* form, the prefix ـبـ /be/ will be "replaced"

with the prefix نـَ /na/.

EXAMPLES:

- *positive* form:

Sit!   /be.ne.šin/ بِنِشین!

- *negative* form:

Don't sit!   /na.ne.šin/ نَنِشین!

The table below contains the *tense prefixes* in their *positive* and *negative* forms.

Tense Prefixes (Positive & Negative Forms)
(Table 10.3)

Tense Prefix (Negative Form) added to the beginning of the *Main Verb*	Tense Prefix (Positive Form) added to the beginning of the *Main Verb*	Tenses
نمی	می	Simple Present
نَـ	بِـ	Present Subjunctive
n/a	می	Present Progressive
نَـ	–	Simple Past
نمی	می	Imperfect Indicative
نَـ	–	Present Perfect
نَـ	–	Past Perfect
نَـ	–	Past Subjunctive
n/a	می	Past Progressive
نَـ added to the beginning of the Auxiliary Verb	–	Simple Future
نَـ	– or بِـ	Command

Note:

When the *negative prefix* نَـ /na/ is added to the beginning of a verb that in its infinitive form starts with the letter آ /ă/, the letter آ /ă/ will change into ا /ă/ and the *negative prefix* نَـ /na/ into نَیـ /nay/.

EXAMPLES:

- *positive* form:

سینا من را آورد.

/si.nă- man- ră- ă.vard/
Sina brought me.

- *negative* form:

سینا من را نَیاورد.

/si.nă- man- ră- na.yă.vard/
Sina did not bring me.

Note:

When the *negative prefix* نَـ /na/ is added to the beginning of an infinitive that starts with any of the three following vowels, the *negative prefix* نَـ /na/ turns into نَیـ /nay/. The vowels also have orthographical changes:

- اُ /o/ ⟶ ُ /o/
- اَ /a/ ⟶ َ /a/
- اِ /e/ ⟶ ِ /e/

EXAMPLES:

to fall /of.tă.dan/ اُفتادن
↓
not to fall /na.yof.tă.dan/ نَیُفتادن

to increase /af.zu.dan/ اَفزودن
↓
not to increase /na.yaf.zu.dan/ نَیَفزودن

to presume /en.găš.tan/ اِنگاشتن
↓
not to presume /na.yen.găš.tan/ نَیِنگاشتن

Chapter 10 – Vocabulary

آ

water	آب
to water	آب دادن
peacefully/slowly	آرام
to meet	آشنا شدن
to create	آفریدن
to come	آمدن
there	آنجا
song	آواز
to bring	آوردن
song	آهنگ

ا

room	اتاق
to need	احتیاج داشتن
Europe	اروپا
to hate/to dislike	از چیزی بد آمدن
to stop working	از کار افتادن
to fall	افتادن
to increase	افزودن
but	اما
to hope	امیدوار بودن
to presume	انگاشتن
to stand	ایستادن

ب

to retell	بازگفتن
to open	باز کردن
to play	بازی کردن
bank	بانک
to believe	باور کردن
child	بچّه
to forgive	بخشیدن
brother	برادر
to pick up	برداشتن
snow	برف
to choose	برگزیدن
to return	برگشتن
to close	بستن
ice cream	بستنی
after	بعد از
to be unlikely to	بعید بودن
louder/taller	بلندتر
to lift up	بلند کردن
shirt	بلوز
stem/root	بن
past stem	بن ماضی
present stem	بن مضارع
to be	بودن
to kiss	بوسیدن
better	بهتر

to put on	به تن کردن
more	بیشتر

پ

to step forward	پا پیش گذاشتن
park	پارک
to cook	پختن
to jump	پریدن
to accept	پذیرفتن
to mail	پست کردن
to give back/ to return	پس دادن
boy/son	پسر
window	پنجره
to wear	پوشیدن
to find	پیدا کردن
suggestion	پیشنهاد
to suggest	پیشنهاد کردن
prefix	پیشوند

ت

to prefer	ترجیح دادن
to thank	تشکّر کردن
to shake	تکان تکان دادن
to call	تلفن زدن
to contact	تماس گرفتن
to finish	تمام کردن
clean	تمیز

to clean	تمیز کردن
faster	تندتر
to be able to/can	توانستن
ball	توپ
to recommend	توصیه کردن

ج

young	جوان

چ

green tea	چایِ سبز

ح

to talk	حرف زدن
truth	حقیقت

خ

house/home	خانه
shopping	خرید
to dry	خشک کردن
to make someone laugh	خنداندن
to laugh	خندیدن
to sleep	خوابیدن
to want	خواستن
to read	خواندن
sister	خواهر
to eat	خوردن

to spill	ریختن		

د

to give	دادن
to have	داشتن
to know	دانستن
daughter/girl	دختر
door/in	در
to hurt	درد کردن
to understand	دریافتن
hand	دست
doctor	دکتر
world	دنیا
again	دوباره
to sew	دوختن
to invite	دعوت کردن
all around	دورتا دور
friend	دوست
to run	دویدن
to see	دیدن
yesterday	دیروز

ر

to cross	رد شدن
to go	رفتن
to dance	رقصیدن
newspaper	روزنامه
on	رویِ

ز

verb tense	زمانِ فعل
early	زود

س

to make/to build	ساختن
quiet	ساکت
next year	سال آینده
to travel	سفر کردن
dog	سگ
apple	سیب

ش

dinner	شام
maybe	شاید
to become	شدن
to wash	شستن
to have doubts	شک داشتن
to break	شکستن
to bloom	شکفتن
to recognize	شناختن
personal suffix (ending)	شناسه
to hear	شنیدن

ص

to talk	صحبت کردن

230

voice/sound	صدا		to drag/to draw	کشیدن
to call on	صدا زدن		key	کلید
			next to	کنارِ

ع

photo/picture	عکس

ف

tomorrow	فردا
to send	فرستادن
to sell	فروختن
verb	فعل
auxiliary verb	فعلِ کمکی
to think	فکر کردن
cup	فنجان
to understand	فهمیدن
movie	فیلم

ق

previously	قبلاً
to walk	قدم زدن
to promise	قول دادن

ک

to work	کار کردن
book	کتاب
library	کتابخانه
to do	کردن
to kill	کشتن

گ

to put	گذاشتن
to cross	گذشتن
to grab/to catch	گرفتن
cat	گربه
cry	گریه
to cry	گریه کردن
to say/to tell	گفتن
flower	گل
to listen	گوش دادن

ل

to be necessary	لازم بودن
clothes	لباس
to shiver	لرزیدن

م

car	ماشین
homework	مشق
infinitive	مصدر
to be possible	ممکن بودن
party	مهمانی
table	میز

ن

letter	نامه
to sit	نشستن
to write	نوشتن
new	نو
to drink	نوشیدن

و

when	وقتی

ه

every day	هر روز
every night	هر شب
right now	همین الآن
weather/air	هوا

ی

someone	یک نفر

Test Yourself:

10.1 Find the **infinitives** within the list of words below and rewrite them in the spaces provided. There are 10 **infinitives** in this exercise.

خوردَم /ḱor.dam/

دادَن /dǎ.dan/

رَقصیدَن /raǧ.si.dan/

خواندَند /ḱǎn.dand/

برداشتیم /bar.dǎš.tim/

دانِستَن /dǎ.nes.tan/

می آمَدی /mi.ǎ.ma.di/

داشتَن /dǎš.tan/

رَفت /raft/

VERBS

كِشیدَن /ke.ši.dan/

خوابیدید /ḱǎ.bi.did/

فکر کَردَن /fekr- kar.dan/

خُشک کَردن /ḱošk- kar.dan/

نَدانَم /na.dǎ.nam/

فَهمیدَن /fah.mi.dan/

بودی /bu.di/

شُدَن /šo.dan/

حرف زَد /harf- zad/

خواستَن /ḱǎs.tan/

دیدَم /di.dam/

Example: دادَن ــــــــــ ١-

‫ـــــــــــــــــــــــــ‬ ‫٢-‬

‫ـــــــــــــــــــــــــ‬ ‫٣-‬

‫ـــــــــــــــــــــــــ‬ ‫٤-‬

‫ـــــــــــــــــــــــــ‬ ‫٥-‬

‫ـــــــــــــــــــــــــ‬ ‫٦-‬

‫ـــــــــــــــــــــــــ‬ ‫٧-‬

‫ـــــــــــــــــــــــــ‬ ‫٨-‬

‫ـــــــــــــــــــــــــ‬ ‫٩-‬

‫ـــــــــــــــــــــــــ‬ ‫١٠-‬

10.2 Break each of the *compound verbs*, *prefix verbs* and *phrasal verbs* into their elements (adjectives, nouns, prepositions, simple verbs…) and write the elements in the spaces provided.

Example:
(to work) /kăr- kar.dan/ ۱- کار کردن

کار _____ + کردن _____

(to talk) /harf- za.dan/ ۲- حرف زدن

_____ + _____

(to come back) /bar.gaš.tan/ ۳- برگشتن

_____ + _____

(to open) /băz- kar.dan/ ۴- باز کردن

_____ + _____

(to dry) /ǩošk- kar.dan/ ۵- خشک کردن

_____ + _____

۶- از کار افتادن /az- kăr- of.tă.dan/ (to stop working)

_____+_____ + _____

۷- باز گفتن /băz- gof.tan/ (to retell)

_____ + _____

۸- پس دادن /pas- dă.dan/ (to return/to give back)

_____ +_____

۹- تکان تکان دادن /te.kăn- te.kăn- dă.dan/ (to shake)

_____+_____ + _____

۱۰- بلند کردن /bo.land- kar.dan/ (to lift up)

_____ + _____

10.3 In the exercise below, write the **past stem** of each **verb** in the space provided.

Example: to sit   /ne.šas.tan/ نِشَستن –١

نِشَست

to cross   /go.zaš.tan/ گُذشتن –٢

_____

to go   /raf.tan/ رفتن –٣

_____

to say   /gof.tan/ گفتن –۴

_____

to be able to   /ta.vă.nes.tan/ توانستن –۵

_____

to want   /ḱăs.tan/ خواستن –۶

_____

۷- دیدن /di.dan/   to see

_____

۸- شنیدن /še.ni.dan/   to hear

_____

۹- بستن /bas.tan/   to close

_____

۱۰- پختن /poǩ.tan/   to cook

_____

۱۱- دوختن /duǩ.tan/   to sew

_____

۱۲- آمدن /ǎ.ma.dan/   to come

_____

10.4

In this exercise, change the **present stem** of each **verb** into its **infinitive** form and write it in the space provided.

Example: ۱- بوس /bus/

بوسیدن

۲- رقص /raĝs/

۳- خواب /ḱăb/

۴- خند /ḱand/

۵- خوان /ḱăn/

۶- خور /ḱor/

۷- نوش /nuš/

۸- پوش /puš/

۹- خر /ḱar/

۱۰- شِکُف /še.kof/

_____

۱۱- پَر /par/

_____

10.5 Change each of the following verbs into a **past participle** (objective adjective) using the **past stem** and the suffix ‫ه — ه‬ /e/ . Write the elements in the spaces provided.

Example: to do   /kar.dan/ ۱- کردن

کرده = ه + کرد

to eat   /ǩor.dan/ ۲- خوردن

_____ = _____ + _____

to see   /di.dan/ ۳- دیدن

_____ = _____ + _____

to break   /še.kas.tan/ ۴- شکستن

_____ = _____ + _____

241

۵- گفتن /gof.tan/   to say

_____ = _____ + _____

۶- نشستن /ne.šas.tan/   to sit

_____ = _____ + _____

۷- ایستادن /is.tǎ.dan/   to stand

_____ = _____ + _____

۸- بودن /bu.dan/   to be

_____ = _____ + _____

۹- رفتن /raf.tan/   to go

_____ = _____ + _____

۱۰- پختن /poǩ.tan/   to cook

_____ = _____ + _____

۱۱- داشتن /dǎš.tan/   to have

_____ = _____ + _____

۱۲- خواستن /ǩǎs.tan/   to want

_____ = _____ + _____

10.6 Rewrite each sentence below, changing the **verbs** from the **simple present tense** into the **simple past tense.** (The infinitive form of each verb is shown in the parentheses to help you conjugate the verb.)

Example:

۱- من با تو بازی می کنم. (بازی کردن)

/man- bă- to- bă.zi- mi.ko.nam/

I play with you.

من با تو بازی کردم.

۲- سارا اینجا می نشیند. (نشستن)

/să.ră- in.jă- mi.ne.ši.nad/

Sara sits here.

۳- پسرم در اُتاقش می خوابد. (خوابیدن)

/pe.sa.ram- dar- o.tă.ğaš- mi.ẍă.bad/

My son sleeps in his room.

۴- من کتاب ها را روی میزِ می گذارم. (گذاشتن)

/man- ke.tăb.hă- ră- ru.ye- miz- mi.go.ză.ram/

I put the books on the table.

۵- شما با ما می آیید. (آمدن)

/šo.mă- bă- mă- mi.ă.yid/

You come with us.

10.7 Rewrite the sentences below, changing the **verbs** from the **present perfect tense** into the **past perfect tense**.

Example:

۱- پدرم از سفر برگشته است.

/pe.da.ram- az- sa.far- bar.gaš.te- ast/

My father has returned from the trip.

پدرم از سفر برگشته بود.

۲- مادرم با مادرت آشنا شده است.

/mă.da.ram- bă- mă.da.rat- ă.še.nă- šo.de- ast/

My mother has met your mother.

۳- ما یک ماشینِ نو خریده ایم.

/mă- yek- mă.ši.ne- no- ǩa.ri.de.im/

We have bought a new car.

۴- من سارا را دعوت کرده ام.

/man- să.ră- ră- da'.vat- kar.de.am/
I have invited Sara.

۵- خواهرهایم تو را در کتابخانه دیده اند.

/kă.har.hă.yam- to- ră- dar- ke.tăb.kă.ne- di.de.and/
My sisters have seen you in the library.

10.8 Rewrite the sentences below, changing the **verbs** from the **present progressive tense** into the **past progressive tense**.

Example:

۱- من دارم روزنامه می خوانم.

/man- dă.ram- ruz.nă.me- mi.kă.nam/
I am reading the newspaper.

من داشتم روزنامه می خواندم.

۲- تو داری می لرزی.

/to- dă.ri- mi.lar.zi/
You are shivering.

٣- آنها دارند خوب می رقصند.

/ăn.hă- dă.rand- ǩub- mi.rağ.sand/
They are dancing well.

_____

٤- سارا دارد دخترش را صدا می زند.

/să.ră- dă.rad- doǩ.ta.raš- ră- se.dă- mi.za.nad/
Sara is calling on her daughter.

_____

٥- ما داریم شما را دعوت می کنیم.

/mă- dă.rim- šo.mă- ră- da'.vat- mi.ko.nim/
We are inviting you.

_____

10.9 In each example below, there is a **verb** in **infinitive** form and another word in parentheses. Using these words, write two sentences to provide a **command**.

Example:

١- (آرام - خوابیدن)

/ǩă.bi.dan/ - /ă.răm/
(to sleep – peacefully)

آرام بخواب!

آرام بخوابید!

۲- (بلندتر - خواندن)

/k̆ăn.dan/ - /bo.land.tar/
(to read – louder)

_____

_____

۳- (آب - نوشیدن)

/nu.ši.dan/ - /ăb/
(to drink – water)

_____

_____

۴- (تندتر - رقصیدن)

/rağ.si.dan/ - /tond.tar/
(to dance – faster)

_____

_____

۵- (بیشتر - خندیدن)

/k̆an.di.dan/ - /biš.tar/
(to laugh – more)

_____

_____

$\mathbb{10.10}$ Read each sentence below. Change the **verb** in each sentence from the **simple past tense** into the **simple future tense**, using the auxiliary verb خواستن /ǩǎs.tan/. Rewrite each sentence in the space provided.

Example:

۱– من با تو حرف زدم.

/man- bǎ- to- harf- za.dam/
I talked to you.

من با تو حرف خواهم زد.

۲– تو فنجان را شکستی.

/to- fen.jǎn- rǎ- še.kas.ti/
You broke the cup.

_____

۳– رایان دوباره ایستاد.

/rǎ.yǎn- do.bǎ.re- is.tǎd/
Ryan stood up again.

_____

۴– ما ظرف ها را شستیم.

/mǎ- zarf.hǎ- rǎ- šos.tim/
We washed the dishes.

_____

۵– شما حقیقت را گفتید.

/šo.mǎ- ha.ǧi.ǧat- rǎ- gof.tid/
You told the truth.

10.11
Look at the list of words below. Identify and underline the **transitive verbs**. Then, use each **transitive verb** to write a sentence in the **simple present tense** with the help of the **object** provided for each sentence. There are 5 **transitive verbs** in this exercise.

Example: to eat   /ǩor.dan/ <u>خوردن</u>

to bloom   /še.kof.tan/ شکُفتن

to fall   /of.tǎ.dan/ اُفتادن

to laugh   /ǩan.di.dan/ خندیدن

to sell   /fo.ruǩ.tan/ فُروختن

to tell   /gof.tan/ گفتن

to pick up   /bar.dǎš.tan/ برداشتن

to hear   /še.ni.dan/ شنیدن

to sit   /ne.šas.tan/ نشستن

249

VERBS

to stand /is.tă.dan/ ایستادن

۱- من سیب /sib/ (apple) را ــــــــــ می خورم .

۲- تو خانه /kă.ne/ (house) را ـــــــــــــ .

۳- ما حقیقت /ha.ği.ğat/ (truth) را ـــــــــــــ .

۴- آنها کتاب ها /ke.tăb.hă/ (books) را ـــــــــــــ .

۵- او صدا /se.dă/ (voice) را ـــــــــــــ .

10.12 Rewrite the sentences below, changing the **active voice** of the **verb** into the **passive voice.** The infinitive form of each verb has been provided in parentheses to guide you.

Example:

۱- من بستنی را خوردم. (خوردن)
/man- bas.ta.ni- ră- ğor.dam/
I ate the ice cream.

بستنی خورده شد.

۲- دوستانم فیلم را دیدند. (دیدن)

/dus.tă.nam- film- ră- di.dand/
My friends saw the movie.

۳- ما ماشین ها را شستیم. (شستن)

/mă- mă.šin.hă- ră- šos.tim/
We washed the cars.

۴- الیزابت نامه را پُست کرد. (پُست کردن)

/e.li.ză.bet- nă.me- ră- post- kard/
Elizabeth mailed the letter.

۵- تو گُل ها را آب دادی. (آب دادن)

/to- gol.hă- ră- ăb- dă.di/
You watered the flowers.

10.13 Add the appropriate prefix to the beginning of each of the following **verbs** to change it into its **negative** form. Then, rewrite the **verb** in the space provided.

Example:.   ۱- خشک می کردند.

/kŏšk- mi.kar.dand/

[They] were drying. / [They] used to dry

خشک + نِ + می کردند. = خشک نِمی کردند.

۲- می فهمم.

/mi.fah.mam/

[I] understand.

_____ = _____ + ____

۳- شکست.

/še.kast/

[It] broke.

_____ = _____ + ____

۴- اُفتاده ام.

/of.tă.de.am/

[I] have fallen.

_____ = ____ + _____ + ____

۵- فراموش کرده بودند.

/fa.ră.muš- kar.de- bu.dand/
[They] had forgotten.

_____ = _____ + _____ + ____ + _____

۶- بنشین!

/be.ne.šin/
Sit!

_____ = _____ + ____

۷- شاید پُخته باشد.

/šă.yad- poǩ.te- bă.šad/
[He/She] might have cooked.

_____ = _____ + _____ + ____ + _____

۸- شاید بیایند.

/šă.yad- bi.yă.yand/
[They] might come.

_____ = _____ + ____ + _____

٩- خواهید دانست.

/kă.hid- dă.nest/
[You] will know.

_____ = _____ + _____ + _____

١٠- بر می گردیم.

/bar.mi.gar.dim/
[We] return.

_____ = _____ + ____ + _____

١١- پیدا خواهند کرد.

/pey.dă- kă.hand- kard/
[They] will find.

_____ = ____ + _____ + ___ + _____

١٢- گریه می کردم.

/ger.ye- mi.kar.dam/
[I] cried./ [I] used to cry.

_____ = _____ + ____ + _____

۱۳ – تمیز شده است.

/ta.miz- šo.de- ast/
[It] has been cleaned.

_____ = _____ + _____ + _____ + _____

۱۴ – آمد.

/ă.mad/
[He/She] came.

_____ = _____ + _____

۱۵ – دیده شد.

/di.de- šod/
[It] was seen.

_____ = _____ + _____ + _____

255

KEYS TO EXERCISES

Chapter 1: Nouns

1.1

۱- گل + دان ۲- روان + شناس + ی ۳- کتاب + خانه ۴- زد + و + خورد

۵- پست + خانه

1.2

۱- سارا میوه ۲- کتاب ها میز ۳- خانه سینا تهران

۴- خنده سارا ۵- میز سارا کتاب هیمالیا ۶- گلدان دختر

۷- ماه آسمان تهران ۸- خیابان درخت

1.3

۱- دخترها دختران ۲- جانور ها جانوران ۳- سبزی ها سبزیجات

۴- درخت ها درختان ۵- عدد ها اعداد ۶- خواننده ها خوانندگان

۷- موج ها امواج ۸- نویسنده ها نویسندگان ۹- ماه ها

۱۰- ترانه ها

1.4

دانشجو (cn) الیزابت (pn) فرانسه (pn) خانه (cn) گل (cn) حیوان (cn)

سارا (pn) مکزیک (pn) فروردین (pn) شوهر (cn) میز (cn) ماه (cn) پاریس (pn)

نیویورک (pn)   خیابان (cn)   پنجره (cn)   کریسمس (pn)   بانو (cn)   دختر (cn)

نوروز (pn)   ترانه (cn)

1.5

گریه ✓   کاهش ✓   خواهش ✓   خواننده ✓   خنده ✓   گفتار ✓

نوشتار ✓

1.6

۲- خانه ای   یک خانه   یک خانه ای   ۱- گربه ای   یک گربه   یک گربه ای

۴- میزی   یک میز   یک میزی   ۳- درختی   یک درخت   یک درختی

۶- دخترانی   ۷- نویسندگانی   ۵- دریایی   یک دریا   یک دریایی

۹- بوسه ای   یک بوسه   یک بوسه ای   ۸- کوهی   یک کوه   یک کوهی

۱۱- گریه ای   یک گریه   یک گریه ای   ۱۰- کتاب هایی

۱۳- پنجره هایی   ۱۲- تپّه ای   یک تپّه   یک تپّه ای

۱۶- خنده ای   یک خنده   یک خنده ای   ۱۴- اسم هایی   ۱۵- سبزیجاتی

Chapter 2: Pronouns

2.1

۳- آنها به دیدنِ من آمدند.   ۲- ما به پارک می رویم.   ۱- او دیروز از سفر برگشت.

۵- شما جوان هستید.   ۴- او دخترِ خیلی زیبایی ست.

2.2

۲- من او را خیلی دوست دارم.   ۱- سینا آنها را به سفر می برد.

۴- من شما را به خانه ام دعوت کردم.   ۳- مادرم ما را در رستوران دید.

۶- فردا آنها را به سفر خواهم برد.   ۵- الیزابت او را به پارک بُرد.

۸- سینا دارد او را می بوسد.   ۷- ما او را به لندن فرستادیم.

2.3

۲- ما به سختی آنها را شناختیم.   ۱- من دیروز تو را در پارک دیدم.

۴- سارا من را دوست دارد.   ۳- پدرش با خوشحالی او را بوسید.

۶- او را صدا کردم.   ۵- مادر سینا ما را به خانه آورد.

۸- من برای امتحان آنها را آماده کردم.   ۷- سینا من را در آغوش کشید.

2.4

۲- با خوشحالی به او غذا دادم.   ۱- به تو گفتم: «بیا !»

۴- با احترام به تو جواب دادم.   ۳- فارسی را به شما یاد دادم.

۶- باشوق به او نگاه کردم.   ۵- خانه را به آنها نشان دادم.

2.5

۲- ماشینِ آنها خیلی قدیمی است.   ۱- کیفِ او قرمز است.

۴- سارا، دوستِ ما است.   ۳- کفش های شما زیبا هستند.

۶- دست های شما خیس هستند.   ۵- کتاب های آنها سنگین هستند.

۸- آپارتمانِ او در طبقه ی دوّم است.   ۷- مدرسه ی ما از اینجا خیلی دور است.

2.6

۲- ما کشورتان را دوست داریم. ۱- من می خواهم با خواهرَت برقصم.

۴- دخترهایمان در لندن زندگی می کنند. ۳- تو کیفَم را گم کردی.

۶- ماشین هایشان نو هستند. ۵- گلدانَم افتاد و شکست.

۸- دوستانتان دوست دارند آواز بخوانند. ۷- سگَش خیلی می خوابد.

2.7

۱- من دوست دارم درباره ی خودَم بنویسم.

۲- آنها باید این مشکل را خودشان حل کنند.

۳- تو باید از خودَت بپرسی که کدام شغل را بیشتر دوست داری.

۴- شما باید از خودتان خجالت بکشید!

۵- ما می توانیم به خودمان کمک کنیم.

۶- او بهتر از هرکسی خودَش را می شناسد.

2.8

۲- این ماشینِ قرمز، مالِ ما است. ۱- این سیب مالِ من است.

۴- تو مالِ او را خوردی. ۳- من مالِ تو را برداشتم.

۶- مریم مالِ تو را پوشیده است. ۵- مالِ شما از مالِ آنها نوتر است.

۸- این کلید، مالِ من نیست. ۷- مالِ من بهتر از مالِ تو است.

۹- کیفی که پیدا کردی، مالِ ما بود.

Chapter 3: Adjectives

3.1

۱- خوش + قلب ۲- با +هوش ۳- دوست + داشتن + ی

۴- بی + شرم ۵-بخش + نده ۶- نا + آرام

۷- مهمان + نواز ۸- بی + ارزش ۹- آفتاب + ی

۱۰- باور +نکردن + ی

3.2

۱- دوست داشتنی ۲- خوردنی ۳- دیدنی ۴- خواندنی ۵-شنیدنی

۶- باور کردنی ۷- باور نکردنی ۸- ماندنی ۹- پرستیدنی ۱۰-شکستنی

۱۱-مُردنی ۱۲-گفتنی ۱۳- خواستنی ۱۴- عوض کردنی ۱۵- دور انداختنی

3.3

۱- تابان ۲- خندان ۳- نالان ۴- لنگان ۵- ترسان ۶- لرزان

3.4

۱- خانه ی ما بزرگ ترین خانه ی این کوچه است. ۲- فرانسه یک کشورِ اُروپایی است.

۳- دخترت بسیار زیبا است. ۴- رنگِ برف سفید است.

۵- شاخه ی آن درخت شکسته است.

3.5

۲- این کتابِ به زبانِ انگلیسی است.   ۱- شوهرِ من آمریکایی است.

۳- من دوست دارم زبان فارسی را یاد بگیرم.

۴- یادگیریِ زبانِ ایتالیایی از زبانِ آلمانی ساده تر است.

۶- ایران یک کشورِ آسیایی است.   ۵- من دوستانِ مکزیکی بسیاری دارم.

۷- من کانادایی هستم.

3.6

۶- شنیده   ۵- گفته   ۴- دیده   ۳- خورده   ۲- بسته   ۱- شکسته

۱۱- آلوده   ۱۰- پخته   ۹- رفته   ۸- کرده   ۷- مانده

3.7

۱- بزرگ تر   ۲- کوچک تر   ۳- سفیدتر   ۴- سیاه تر   ۵- شکسته تر

۶- شادتر   ۷- آرام تر   ۸- بلندتر   ۹- نرم تر   ۱۰- زیباتر   ۱۱- تابان تر

Chapter 4: Adverbs

4.1

۱- هرگز   ۲- دیشب   دیر   ۳- خوشبختانه   امروز

۴- دیروز   احتمالاً   با خوشحالی   ۵- همیشه   تنها   ۶- فردا   زود

۷- سریع   خوب   ۸- بدونِ تردید   امروز

4.2

۱– شاگردانِ من صبورانه منتظرِ من بودند.

۲– آنها شجاعانه با دشمن جنگیدند.

۳– ما مشتاقانه برای سفرمان به ترکیه برنامه ریختیم.

۴– سارا خوشبختانه در تصادف زخمی نشده است.

۵– دخترِ من آگاهانه این تصمیم را گرفته است.

۶– سینا هشیارانه به من گوش داد.

۷– تو هنرمندانه آشپزی می کنی.

۸– با ما بسیار محترمانه رفتار کردند.

4.3

۲– بچّه ها به زودی از اتاق بیرون خواهند آمد. ۱– پسرم دیروز مشکل را به من گفت.

۴– سینا گاهی به من تلفن می زند. ۳– من دیشب کلید را به آن مرد دادم.

۵– پستچی هر روز جعبه ها را روی زمین می گذارد.

4.4

۲– سام حتماً به من کمک می کند. ۱– ما هفته ی گذشته از سفر برگشتیم.

۴– متأسّفانه پدرم به ایران برگشت. ۳– سارا به تنهایی تمامِ ظرف ها را شست.

۶ – من از شما حقیقتاً معذرت می خواهم. ۵– سینا باشوق هدیه اش را باز کرد.

۷- پدر و مادرم به آرامی در را باز کردند. ۸- من کمی دلم برای سارا تنگ شده است.

۹- برادرم دیر به خانه آمد. ۱۰- ماشینِ من خوب کار می کند.

Chapter 5: Prepositions

5.1

۱- از به ۲- به جز ۳- در با ۴- از تا با

۵- برایِ ۶- در از برایِ ۷- از در

Chapter 6: Conjunctions

6.1

۱- و ۲- به محضی که و ۳- و امّا

۴- و امّا چون ۵- در حالی که ۶- و در نتیجه

۷- و ولی ۸- وقتی و

Chapter 7: Kasre-ye Ezăfe

7.1

۱- مادر بزرگِ من پیر است. ۲- کلاسِ ما فردا شروع می شود.

۳- ماشینِ شما خراب است. ۴- گردنبندِ تو از طلاست.

۵- من دیروز کتابِ تو را پس دادم. ۶- مدادِ او شکست.

۷- خانه ی آنها دور است. ۸- پنجره های من باز هستند.

۹- مویِ شما بلندست. ۱۰- دندانِ او درد می کند.

۱۱- کیفِ ما سنگین است.

Chapter 8: Direct Object Indicator

8.1

۱- پدر و مادرم تو را به مهمانی شان دعوت کرده اند.

۲- باید تمام ظرفِ ها را بشویم.   ۳- دوست داری پیراهنِ تازه ی من را ببینی؟

۴- دوست آمریکاییِ من، زبانِ فارسی را دوست دارد.

۵- امروز مدرسه ها را تعطیل کرده اند.   ۶- کتابت را به من قرض می دهی؟

۷- فراموش کردم کامپیوترم را بیاورم.   ۸- هنوز مقاله ام را تایپ نکرده ام.

۹- ما مریم را دیدیم.   ۱۰- دوستانم دوربینِ من را پیدا نکردند.

۱۱- گردنبندت را پس دادم.

Chapter 9: Arabic Signs

9.1

۴-اساساً   ۳- دقیقاً   ۲- لطفاً   ۱- فوراً

۸- شدیداً   ۷-حقیقتاً   ۶- احتمالاً   ۵- تماماً

9.2

۴-مسأله   ۳- رئیس   ۲- مسئول   ۱- مؤدّب

۸- متأسّفانه   ۷- پائیز   ۶- سؤال   ۵- مؤثّر

9.3

۱- نقّاش　　۲- تپّه　　۳- سکّه　　۴- تکّه　　۵- عکّاس　　۶- محقّق

۷- تفکّر　　۸- تخیّل　　۹- تمدّن　　۱۰- مقصّر　　۱۱- معلّم　　۱۲- توجّه

۱۳- مجسّمه　　۱۴- بچّه　　۱۵- محبّت

Chapter 10: Verbs

10.1

۱- دادَن　　۲- رقصیدَن　　۳- دانِستَن　　۴- داشتَن　　۵- کِشیدَن

۶- فکر کردَن　　۷- خشک کردَن　　۸- فهمیدَن　　۹- شدَن　　۱۰- خواستَن

10.2

۱- کار + کردن　　۲- حرف + زدن　　۳- بر + گشتن　　۴- باز + کردن

۵- خشک + کردن　　۶- از + کار + افتادن　　۷- باز + گفتن

۸- پس + دادن　　۹- تکان + تکان + دادن　　۱۰- بلند + کردن

10.3

۱- نشست　　۲- گذشت　　۳- رفت　　۴- گفت　　۵- توانست

۶- خواست　　۷- دید　　۸- شنید　　۹- بست　　۱۰- پخت

۱۱- دوخت　　۱۲- آمد

10.4

۱- بوسیدن　　۲- رقصیدن　　۳- خوابیدن　　۴- خندیدن　　۵- خواندن

۶- خوردن　　۷- نوشیدن　　۸- پوشیدن　　۹- خریدن　　۱۰- شکفتن

۱۱- پریدن

10.5

۱- کرد + ه = کرده   ۲- خورد + ه = خورده   ۳- دید + ه = دیده

۴- شکست + ه = شکسته   ۵- گفت + ه = گفته   ۶- نشست + ه = نشسته

۷- ایستاد + ه = ایستاده   ۸- بود + ه = بوده   ۹- رفت + ه = رفته

۱۰- پخت + ه = پخته   ۱۱- داشت + ه = داشته   ۱۲- خواست + ه = خواسته

10.6

۱- من با تو بازی کردم.   ۲- سارا اینجا نشست.   ۳- پسرم در اتاقش خوابید.

۴- من کتاب ها را روی میز گذاشتم.   ۵- شما با ما آمدید.

10.7

۱- پدرم از سفر برگشته بود.   ۲- مادرم با مادرت آشنا شده بود.

۳- ما یک ماشینِ نو خریده بودیم.   ۴- من سارا را دعوت کرده بودم.

۵- خواهرهایم تو را در کتابخانه دیده بودند.

10.8

۱- من داشتم روزنامه می خواندم.   ۲- تو داشتی می لرزیدی.

۳- آنها داشتند خوب می رقصیدند.   ۴- سارا داشت دخترش را صدا می زد.

۵- ما داشتیم شما را دعوت می کردیم.

10.9

۱- آرام بخواب! / آرام بخوابید!   ۲- بلندتر بخوان! / بلندتر بخوانید!

۳- آب بنوش!/ آب بنوشید!   ۴- تندتر برقص!/ تندتر برقصید!

۵- بیشتر بخند! / بیشتر بخندید!

10.10

۱- من با تو حرف خواهم زد.   ۲- تو فنجان را خواهی شکست.

۳- رایان دوباره خواهد ایستاد.   ۴- ما ظرف ها را خواهیم شست.

۵- شما حقیقت را خواهید گفت.

10.11

۱- من سیب را می خورم.   ۲- تو خانه را می فروشی.   ۳- ما حقیقت را می گوییم.

۴- آنها کتاب ها را برمی دارند.   ۵- او صدا را می شنود.

10.12

۱- بستنی خورده شد.   ۲- فیلم دیده شد.   ۳- ماشین ها شسته شدند.

۴- نامه پست شد.   ۵- گل ها آب داده شدند.

10.13

۱- خشک + نِ + می کردند = خشک نِمی کردند.   ۲- نِ + می فهمم = نِمی فهمم.

۳- نَ + شکست = نَشکست.   ۴- نَیـ + اُفتاده + ام = نَیُفتاده ام.

۵- فراموش + نَ + کرده + بودند = فراموش نَکرده بودند.   ۶- نَ + نِشین = نَنِشین!   ۷-
شاید + نَ + پخته + باشد = شاید نَپخته باشد.   ۸- شاید + نَیـ + آیند = شاید نَیایند.

‏۱۰- بر + نـ + می گردیم = بر نِمی گردیم.‏ ‏۹- نَ + خواهید + دانست = نَخواهید دانست.‏

‏۱۱- پیدا + نَ + خواهند + کرد = پیدا نَخواهند کرد.‏

‏۱۲- گریه + نِ + می کردم = گریه نِمی کردم.‏

‏۱۴- نَیـ + آمد = نَیامد.‏ ‏۱۳- تَمیز + نَ + شده + است = تمیز نَشده است.‏

‏۱۵- دیده + نَ + شد = دیده نَشد.‏

References:

- انوری، حسن و احمدی گیوی، حسن . دستور زبان فارسی ۱، انتشارات فاطمی، ویرایش چهارم، چاپ دوم، ۱۳۹۱، تهران

- احمدی گیوی، حسن و انوری، حسن. دستور زبان فارسی ۲، انتشارات فاطمی، ویرایش چهارم، چاپ دوم، ۱۳۹۱، تهران

- ناتل خانلری، پرویز. دستور زبان فارسی، انتشارات توس، چاپ بیست و سوم، ۱۳۹۱ ، تهران

Similar Titles

Laugh and Learn
Persian Idioms
Nazanin Mirsadeghi

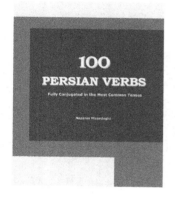

100
Persian Verbs
(Fully Conjugated in the Most Common Tenses)
Nazanin Mirsadeghi

1000 +
Most Useful
Persian Words
Nazanin Mirsadeghi

100
Irregular
Persian Verbs
(Fully Conjugated in the Most Common Tenses)
Nazanin Mirsadeghi

500+
Persian Phrases
Daily Conversations for better Communication

Nazanin Mirsadeghi

Persian Folktale

Once Upon a Time
(Seven Persian Folktales)
Persian/Farsi Edition
Meimanat Mirsadeghi (Zolghadr)

To Learn More about BAHAR BOOKS

Please Visit the Website :

www.baharbooks.com

Bahar Books

Made in United States
Orlando, FL
05 October 2022

23020383R10150